Log Cabin
Restructured

First Published in the United States of America in 2014 by Fons & Porter Books, an imprint of F+W Media, Inc., 10151 Carver Road, Suite 200, Blue Ash, Ohio 45242. (800) 289-0963. First Edition.

www.fwmedia.com

17 16 15 14 13   5 4 3 2 1

Original Japanese edition published by NHK Publishing, Inc., Japan
KUROHA SHIZUKO NO QUILT JIYUJIZAI NI LOG CABIN
Copyright © 2008 Shizuko Kuroha
All rights reserved.

This English edition is published by arrangement with
NHK Publishing, Inc., through Tuttle-Mori Agency, Inc., Tokyo

English language rights, translation & production by World Book Media, LLC
Email: info@worldbookmedia.com
Translator: Atsuko Imanishi

Distributed in Canada by Fraser Direct
100 Armstrong Avenue
Georgetown, ON, Canada L7G 5S4
Tel: (905) 877-4411

Distributed in the U.K. and Europe by F&W MEDIA INTERNATIONAL
Brunel House, Newton Abbot, Devon, TQ12 4PU, England
Tel: (+44) 1626 323200, Fax: (+44) 1626 323319
Email: enquiries@fwmedia.com

Distributed in Australia by Capricorn Link
P.O. Box 704, S. Windsor NSW, 2756 Australia
Tel: (02) 4560 1600, Fax: (02) 4577 5288
E-mail: books@capricornlink.com.au

ISBN-13: 978-1-4402-4155-0
SRN: T2548

Manufactured in China

Log Cabin Restructured

23 Log Cabin Quilt Projects Made with Triangles, Diamonds, Hexagons and Curves

Shizuko Kuroha

CINCINNATI, OH

INTRODUCTION

The log cabin motif is one of my most favorite patchwork designs. The blocks themselves are simple to sew and can be combined to create a nearly endless number of intricate patterns. When designing, I often find inspiration in beautiful antique quilts. The log cabin motif frequently appears in these quilts, suggesting that quilters have been fascinated by this design for centuries.

Over the years, I have made many projects featuring log cabin blocks. Students often admire these designs, but are too intimidated to try one out for themselves. My goal with this book is to quell that unwarranted fear. By mastering a few simple secrets, creating log cabin blocks will be easier than you ever imagined possible.

Once you understand the basics, you can use these techniques to construct log cabin blocks of all shapes and sizes, such as triangles, hexagons, and curves. You can even design your own log cabin variations to create one-of-a-kind quilts.

I hope you enjoy creating the projects included in this book and that you learn something new along the way.

Shizuko Kuroha

CONTENTS

TOOLS

The correct tools make all the difference when quilting. The following guide shows a few of my favorite tools that will assist you in completing the projects featured in this book.

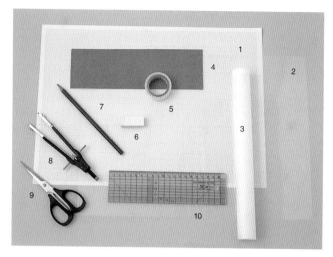

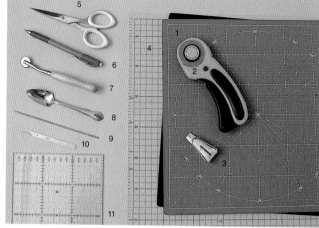

1. **Graph paper:** for drawing block patterns
2. **Mylar sheet:** for making templates
3. **Tracing paper:** for paper piecing and quilting templates
4. **#240 grit sandpaper:** for holding template in place when cutting fabric
5. **Double-sided tape:** for adhering sandpaper to template
6. **Eraser**
7. **Pencil**
8. **Compass**
9. **Paper scissors**
10. **Small ruler**

1. **Rotating cutting mat:** allows you to cut pieces without moving the fabric or your body
2. **Rotary cutter:** use when cutting several pieces at once
3. **Bias tape maker**
4. **Cutting mat:** use a self-healing mat to protect the table when using a rotary cutter
5. **Fabric shears:** can also be used to cut thread
6. **Mechanical marking pencil:** use an erasable pencil
7. **Tracing wheel:** to mark quilting lines
8. **Spoon:** for basting
9. **Stiletto:** to guide fabric and make holes
10. **Seam ripper:** to remove stitches
11. **Quilting ruler:** for cutting fabric

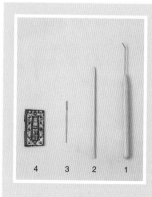

BOUTIS TOOLS

1. **Trapunto needle:** use to fill a quilting channel with stuffing
2. **Boxwood needle:** use this blunt needle to make holes in the fabric
3. **Tapestry needle:** use to insert yarn inside the quilting channel
4. **Fine needles:** use when working with thin fabric

1. **Wrist support glove:** wear on both hands to prevent carpal tunnel syndrome
2. **Needle threader:** threads needles easily
3. **Thimble:** wear resizable thimbles on both hands when quilting
4. **Finger cot:** use to grip needle when quilting
5. **Pins:** use long pins for patchwork and short pins for appliqué
6. **Needles:** use the appropriate size needle for hand piecing, basting, quilting, and whip-stitching
7. **Thread**
   a. **Polyester:** use machine sewing thread for patchwork
   b. **Cotton:** use 100% cotton thread for quilting
   c. **Basting:** easily removed without damaging quilt

A NOTE ON FABRIC

Over her 30 year quilting career, Shizuko Kuroha has grown famous for her use of vintage fabric, specifically indigo. Originally used for clothing worn by peasants during the Edo period of the early 1600s through the mid-1800s, indigo fabric is still popular today and is often used for traditional Japanese quilting and embroidery.

After years of scouring flea markets, Shizuko Kuroha has amassed an impressive collection of vintage fabric. However, the supply of these beautiful textiles is limited, even in Japan. As a result, Shizuko Kuroha also designs reproduction fabrics. In addition to teaching about Japan's history and culture through fabric, she also advises her students on combining vintage and reproduction cloth within the same project.

Many of the projects in this book were made with vintage fabric, such as old kimono cloth. To emulate Shizuko Kuroha's signature style, look for indigo reproduction fabrics, Japanese taupes, and vintage silks.

DRAWING LOG CABIN PATTERNS

You will need to draw your own log cabin patterns for certain projects in this book. Use the following guide to draft your own templates for log cabin blocks of any shape or size.

Basic Log Cabin Block

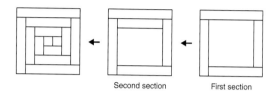

Second section   First section

Draw a square the size of your desired finished block. Working counterclockwise, draw the sections of the block. The size of the center section will vary based on the width of your pieces.

Courthouse Steps Block

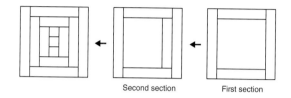

Second section   First section

Draw a square the size of your desired finished block. Draw the sections of the block so that pieces opposite each other are equal in size.

Parallelogram Block

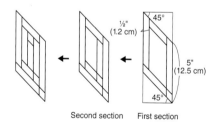

Second section   First section

This example is for a 5" (12.5 cm) parallelogram composed of ½" (1.2 cm) wide strips. Draw a rectangle, then draw 45° lines to make the rectangle into a parallelogram. Fill the parallelogram as shown above.

Diamond Block

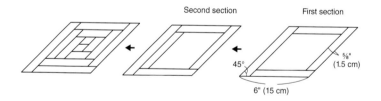

Second section   First section

This example is for a 6" (15 cm) diamond composed of ⅝" (1.5 cm) wide strips. Draw a diamond, then fill the diamond as shown above.

Triangle Block

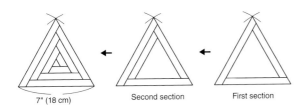

Second section   First section

7" (18 cm)

This example is for a 7" (18 cm) equilateral triangle. Draw a triangle, then fill the triangle as shown above. The size of the center section will vary based on the width of your pieces.

Hexagon Block

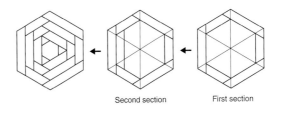

Second section   First section

Use graph paper to draw a hexagon. Fill the hexagon as shown above.

Oval Block

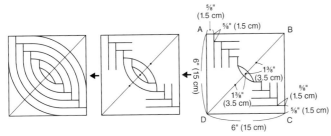

This example is for a 6" (15 cm) oval. Draw a square the size of your desired finished block. Draw $5/8$" (1.5 cm) wide strips at corners A and C. Draw a diagonal line through the block from corners B to D. Position the compass needle along the diagonal line, about $1\,3/8$" (3.5 cm) from the block center. Use the compass to draw a curved line that connects the innermost strips on corners A and C. Follow the same process to connect the remaining strips.

How to Make a Template

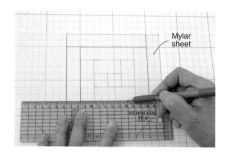

1. Draw a log cabin block following the instructions on page 8. Transfer the pattern onto tracing paper or a mylar sheet to create a template.

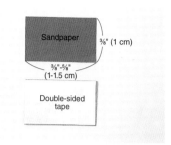

2. Cut out ³⁄₈" x ³⁄₈"-⁵⁄₈" (1 x 1-1.5 cm) rectangles of sandpaper and double-sided tape for each log cabin piece. Adhere one side of the tape to the smooth side of the sandpaper.

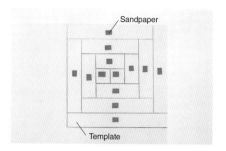

3. Adhere the other side of the tape to the template. Position the tape at the center of the rectangular log cabin pieces and slightly off center for the square pieces. Position the template sandpaper-side down when cutting out fabric.

PATCHWORK BASICS

How to Sew the Pieces Together

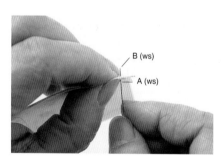

1. Align pieces A and B with right sides together. Both pieces include ¼" (0.6 cm) seam allowance. Insert a pin vertically through both pieces at one of the corner seam allowances.

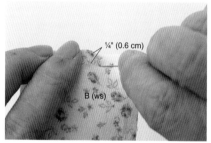

2. Insert the tip of the pin back into the fabric just inside the seam allowance line.

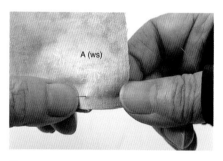

3. Completed view of step 2. The seam allowance lines on pieces A and B should be aligned.

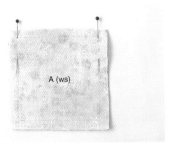

4. Follow the same process to insert a pin at the opposite corner. This technique will allow for easy and accurate hand stitching and the pins will not be in your way.

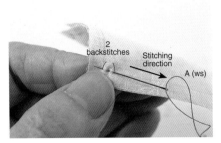

5. Make two backstitches starting at the seam allowance. Do not make a knot.

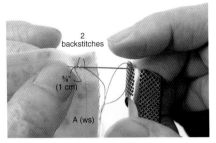

6. Leave a $^3/_8$" (1 cm) long thread tail. Stitch back over the stitches made in step 5.

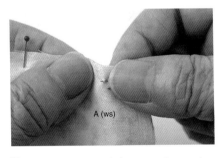

7. Hold the tip of the needle and the fabric between your thumb and index finger. Insert the needle tip through the fabric and draw it out to make one stitch.

8. Push the end of the needle with the thimble on your middle finger. Simultaneously move the fabric in your other hand forward and backward so the needle travels in and out. This is the running stitch.

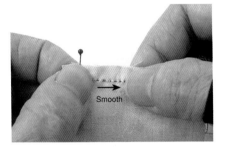

9. Smooth the stitches out between your thumb and index finger. Continue with the running stitch until you reach the end of the line.

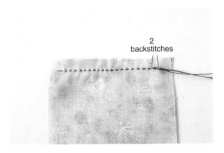

10. Draw the needle out at the corner and smooth the stitches out so they are flat.

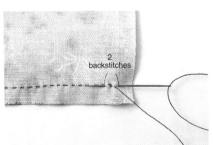

11. Turn the work upside down. Make two backstitches following the same process used in step 5.

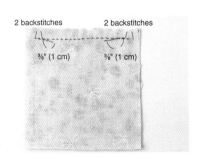

12. Do not make a knot. Clip the thread, leaving a $^3/_8$" (1 cm) long tail.

How to Join Pieces with Intersecting Seams

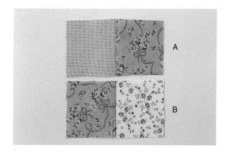

1. Follow the basic patchwork instructions to sew sets A and B.

2. Pin A and B with right sides together. Make two backstitches starting at the seam allowance. Continue stitching until you reach the center. Insert the needle up into the fabric at the right of the center seam allowance. Draw the needle out at the left of the center seam allowance. You have now stitched through the seam allowance diagonally.

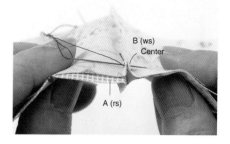

3. Insert the needle through the seam allowance of set B only, traveling back in the direction that you've already stitched.

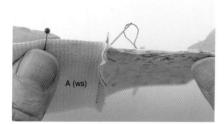

4. Insert the needle down into the fabric at the right of the center seam allowance. Draw the needle out at the left of the center seam allowance. You have now stitched through the seam allowance diagonally in the opposite direction from step 2.

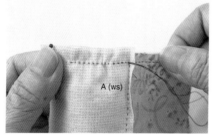

5. Continue stitching until you reach the end of the line. Make two backstitches and clip the thread.

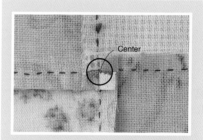

Inserting the needle through the center seam allowance in opposite directions joins four pieces together without forming a hole.

How to Close Up a Hole

When joining several sharply angled pieces together, such as when sewing a star, it may be impossible to avoid a small hole forming at the center. The following guide shows how to close up the hole neatly and securely.

1. Thread a long needle. Insert the eye of the needle through the hole from the wrong side to the right side of the work.

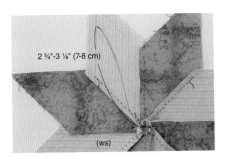

2. Leave a 2 ³/₄"-3 ¹/₈" (7-8 cm) long thread tail.

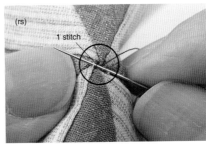

3. Make a small stitch into one of the pointed pieces on the right side of the work.

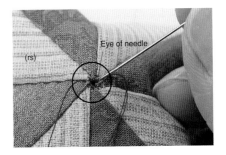

4. Follow the same process to make stitches into each of the remaining seven pieces, whip-stitching the hole closed. Insert the eye of the needle back through the center to the wrong side of the work.

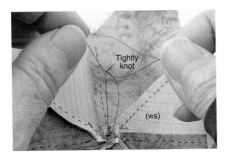

5. Knot the thread tails and trim the excess.

6. Completed view of the closed hole from the right side of the work.

QUILTING BASICS

How to Draw Quilting Lines

This guide uses the Pink Star Tapestry on page 73 as an example; however, the same techniques are used for all projects in this book.

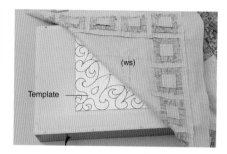

1. Transfer the quilting template from the pattern sheet onto a piece of paper. Position the paper quilting template on a light box. Position the quilt top over the paper quilting template.

2. Pin the paper quilting template to the fabric. Trace the quilting lines onto the fabric using an erasable marking pencil.

How to Baste

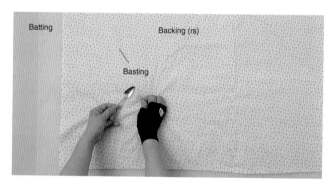

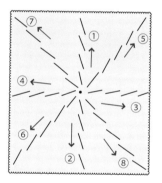

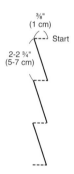

1. Align the backing on top of the batting. Baste the two layers together in a radial pattern, starting at the center and working towards the outside, as shown in the diagrams. Use a large spoon to catch the needle tip when basting.

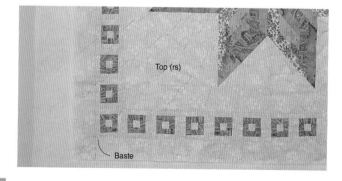

2. Align the quilt top on the other side of the batting. Follow the same process to baste all three layers together in a radial pattern.

How to Quilt

GETTING READY TO QUILT

1. Put a finger cot on the index finger of your dominant hand. This will allow you to grasp the needle firmly. Put thimbles on both hands. Wear a wrist support glove on your dominant hand to prevent carpal tunnel syndrome. I wear my glove inside out so the seam is not in my way.

2. Align the eye of the needle with the tip of the thimble on your dominant hand. Support the needle shaft with your thumb.

3. Hold the needle between your thumb and index finger.

1. Draw a line along the center of each log cabin piece using a tracing wheel. This line will serve as a guide for quilting the log cabin blocks.

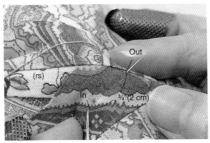

2. Prepare a 15 ³/₄" (40 cm) long thread. Do not knot the thread. Insert the needle into the quilt about ³/₄" (2 cm) away from the starting point. Draw the needle out at the starting point.

3. Leave a ³/₄" (2 cm) long thread tail.

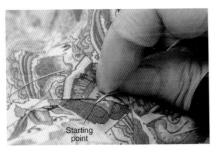

4. Use your left hand to support the quilt from underneath and hold the fabric taut. Insert the tip of the needle through the quilt vertically near the starting point. When the tip of the needle touches the thimble on your left hand, use your right hand to bring the needle tip back up through the quilt layers to the top.

5. Continue inserting the needle tip through the quilt layers and bringing it back up to load 3 more stitches onto the needle.

6. Use the thimbled middle finger of your right hand to push the needle through the fabric.

7. Use your right little finger to hook the thread and pull it towards the starting point.

8. Pull the ¾" (2 cm) long thread tail taut and trim close to the surface of the fabric. The thread tail should now be hidden in the batting.

9. Repeat steps 4-7 to continue quilting along the lines, making four stitches at one time. Always make the same number of stitches at a time for neat and even quilting.

10. To finish quilting, pull the thread in the direction you've already stitched. This will create a small hole in the fabric.

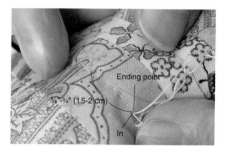

11. Insert the needle through the hole. Bring the needle through the batting for ⅝"-¾" (1.5-2 cm), then draw the needle out on the quilt top. Pull the thread taut and trim close to the surface of the fabric. The thread tail should be hidden among the batting.

How to Bind the Quilt

HOW TO MAKE BIAS TAPE

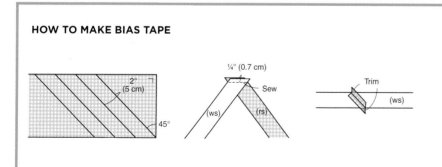

You can make your own bias tape to bind quilts. First, mark your fabric with 45° parallel lines 2" (5 cm) apart and cut into strips. Align the bias strips with right sides together and sew using ¼" (0.7 cm) seam allowance. Trim the excess seam allowance. Sew strips together until bias tape reaches desired length.

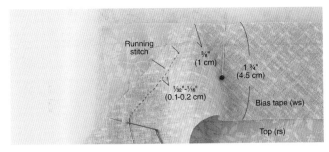

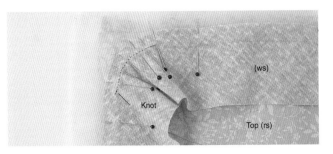

1. Cut out 1 ³/₄" (4.5 cm) wide bias strips (this includes ³/₈" [1 cm] seam allowance). Sew the strips together, as shown on page 16, to create bias tape equal in length to the perimeter of the quilt. With right sides together, pin the bias tape to the raw edges of the quilt. For rounded corners, running stitch the bias tape only ¹/₃₂"-¹/₁₆" (0.1-0.2 cm) inside the seam allowance along the corner portion.

2. Pull the thread tails to gather the bias tape until it fits the curve of the rounded corner, then knot. Use multiple pins to secure the bias tape to the quilt along the rounded corner.

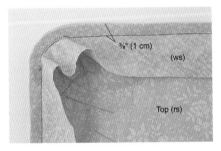

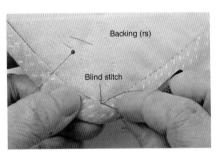

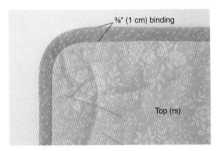

3. Sew the bias tape to the quilt using ³/₈" (1 cm) seam allowance. Trim the excess fabric and batting.

4. Wrap the bias tape around the seam allowance. Blind stitch the bias tape to the backing, covering the line of machine stitching.

5. Completed view of the rounded corner binding from the right side of the quilt.

MITERED CORNER BINDING

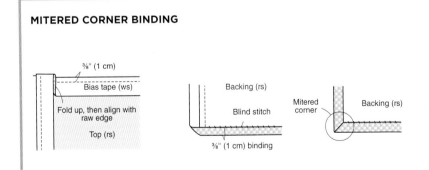

Follow the same process to attach bias tape to the quilt. When you reach the corner seam allowance, fold the bias tape up and away from the quilt at 45°. Crease, then fold the bias tape back down, making a horizontal fold that aligns with the raw edge of the quilt. Continue sewing to attach the bias tape to the quilt, mitering each corner. Wrap the bias tape around the seam allowance and blind stitch to the backing. Refer to pages 18-20 for photos of binding with mitered corners.

How to Bind the Quilt with Piping

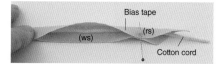

Pre-wash the cotton cord before making the piping to prevent shrinkage.

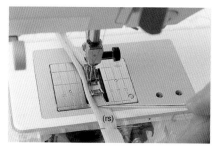

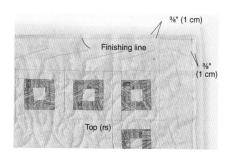

1. Cut out 2" (5 cm) wide bias strips (this includes seam allowance). Sew the strips together, as shown on page 16, to create bias tape equal in length to the perimeter of the quilt. Fold the tape in half widthwise around 1/8" (0.3 cm) diameter cotton cord and pin to secure.

2. Using a zipper presser foot, stitch as close to the cord as possible. Use a stiletto to create a guideline as you sew.

3. Piping should be attached before quilting the borders. Baste the quilt layers together along the borders. Mark the finishing line 3/8" (1 cm) from the raw edge of the quilt top.

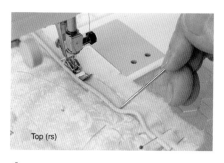

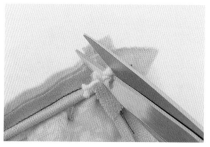

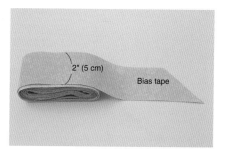

4. Pin the piping to the quilt, aligning the seam from step 2 with the finishing line. Stitch slowly, using a stiletto to fit the piping to the quilt as you sew.

5. Cut the piping when you reach the corner seam allowance. Align a new piece of piping on top and continue sewing around the next side of the quilt. Follow this process to finish sewing around the entire quilt, then trim the excess piping at the corners.

6. Cut out 2" (5 cm) wide bias strips for the binding (this includes seam allowance).

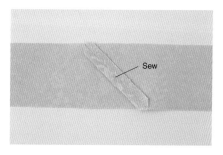

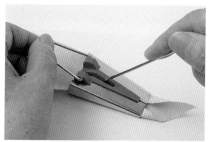

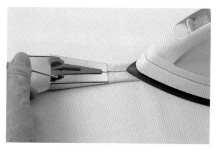

7. Sew the strips together, as shown on page 16, to create bias tape equal in length to the perimeter of the quilt.

8. Insert the bias tape into a 1" (2.5 cm) bias tape maker. Use a stiletto to feed the tape through at the beginning.

9. Press the tape as you draw it out of the bias tape maker. You will now have bias tape that is folded along each long edge.

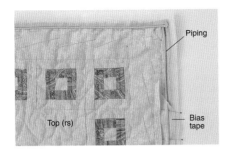

10. Pin the bias tape to the first side of the quilt, aligning one of the folds with the seam from attaching the piping in step 4.

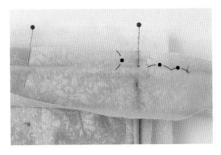

11. Mark the bias tape ³⁄₄" (2 cm) from the corner seam allowance (this distance is equal to double the width of the fold).

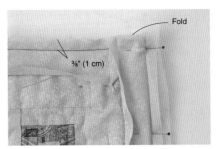

12. Starting 4" (10 cm) from the end, sew the bias tape to quilt. At the corner seam allowance, fold the bias tape up. Crease, then fold the bias tape back down, making a horizontal fold that aligns with the raw edge of the quilt. The mark should align with the corner seam allowance. Pin the bias tape to the quilt along the next side.

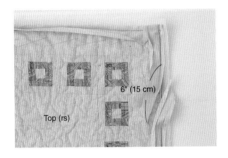

13. Leave the bias strip unattached for the last 6" (15 cm) on the final side of the quilt.

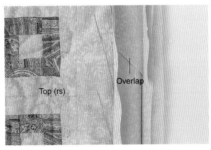

14. Overlap the two ends of the bias tape for the final 6" (15 cm).

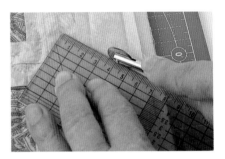

15. Using a ruler and tracing wheel, make a diagonal mark across the overlapped section of the bias tape.

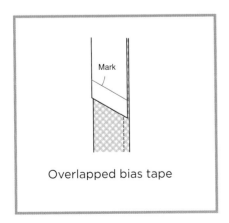

16. With right sides together, sew the bias tape ends along the diagonal mark. Trim the excess fabric, leaving ³⁄₈" (1 cm) seam allowance. Press open.

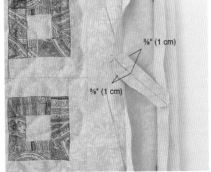

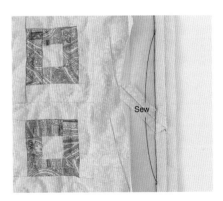

17. Sew the bias tape to the remaining section of the quilt.

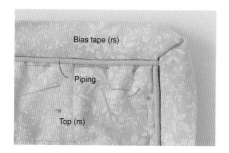

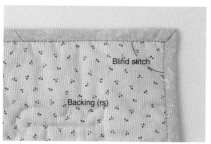

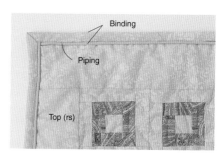

18. Turn the bias tape right side out and adjust the mitered corners.

19. Wrap the bias tape around the seam allowance. Blind stitch the bias tape to the backing.

20. Completed view of piping and binding. Quilt the borders to finish the quilt.

How to Make a Hanging Sleeve

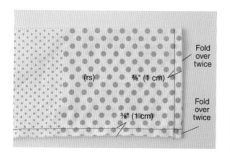

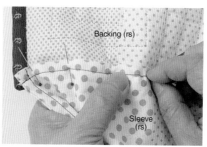

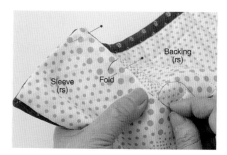

1. Cut a piece of backing fabric 9" (23 cm) x the width of your quilt (this includes seam allowance). Fold the short ends over twice and sew using ⅜" (1 cm) seam allowance. Fold the piece in half with wrong sides together and press. Sew along the long edge using ⅜" (1 cm) seam allowance.

2. Align the long edge seam with the quilt backing, just inside the binding. Hand sew the sleeve to the backing using large stitches. Sew through the backing and batting only, so the stitches are not visible on the right side of the quilt.

3. Fold the sleeve down and pin the folded edge to the backing. Blind stitch through the backing and batting only, so the stitches are not visible on the right side of the quilt.

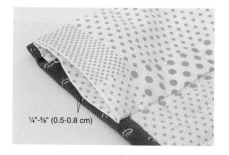

4. Completed view of the hanging sleeve. Insert a bar through the sleeve to hang the quilt. Because the sleeve is positioned about ½" (1.2 cm) below the top of the quilt, the sleeve won't be visible when hung.

PART ONE

Basic Log Cabin Blocks

The projects in this section are constructed with traditional log cabin and courthouse steps blocks. Different fabric layouts are used to create dynamic designs composed entirely from two simple motifs. The technique overviews on pages 32-41 provide detailed instructions and helpful tips on building perfect log cabin blocks.

Courthouse Steps Block

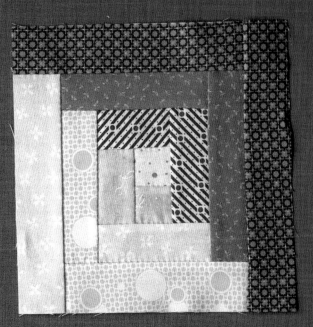

Log Cabin Block

PETITE PIN CUSHIONS

These miniature pin cushions are perfect for storing your finest quality pins and needles. They're constructed with mousseline de laine (a lightweight wool fabric) and wool stuffing to keep those tips sharp and free of rust.

Instructions on page 42

DOUBLE DUTY POT HOLDERS

These elegant pot holders will give you double the delight! The front and back each feature a different log cabin motif; however, they are constructed simultaneously. This technique also works well to create larger pieces, such as reversible chair cushions.

Instructions on page 46

BIAS BLOCK POUCHES

At first glance, this may seem like just another little pouch, but a few unique details make this little piece truly special. A single large log cabin block is oriented on the bias and a zipper is positioned on the curve to lend this pouch a sophisticated look.

Instructions on page 50

DRAWSTRING CUBE BAGS

Although it has a unique shape, this cute and colorful bag is actually quite simple to make. This cube-shaped bag is constructed from five of the same log cabin blocks, so it works up quickly. Use bright colors for a bold statement as shown here, or change the width of the pieces to create a larger bag.

Instructions on page 54

1
2

KIMONO BEDSPREAD

Repurpose vintage kimono cloth to create an elegant and modern bedspread. The silk fabric gives this quilt a luxurious look and feel, but the design also works well in cotton.

Instructions on page 58

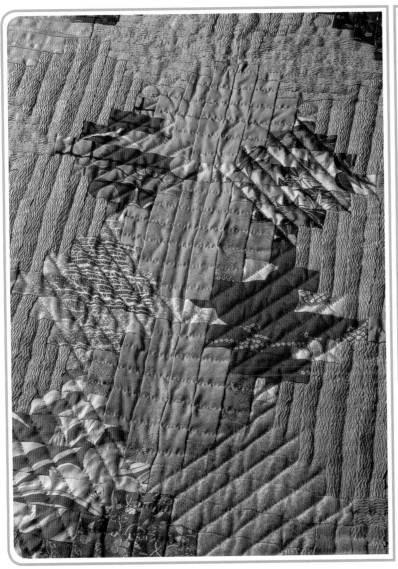

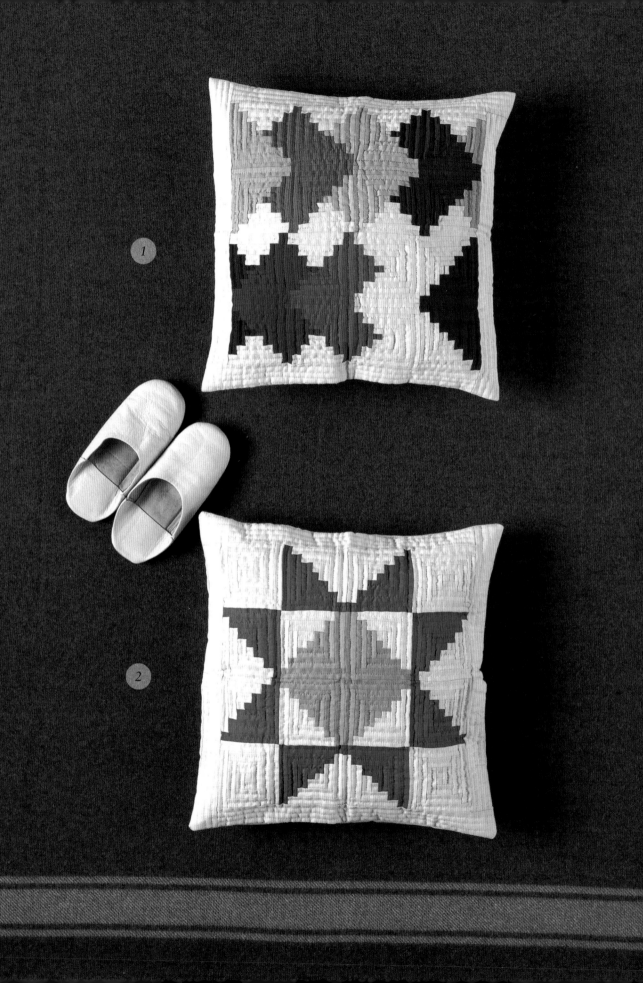

3

PERFECT PATCHWORK PILLOWS

Add a pop of color to your living room with these eye-catching pillows. Each variation is constructed from the same size log cabin blocks, but possesses a unique design based on fabric layout. These patterns also work well for mini quilts...just add a binding!

Instructions on page 61

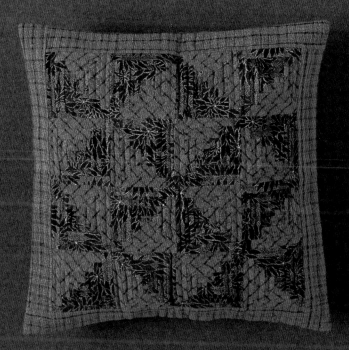

4

SCARLET TAPESTRY

This project is a study in color saturation and dimension. Different shades of red fabric are pieced together to create this subtle, yet dramatic design. Curved bias strips are sandwiched between select log cabin pieces to add a hint of contrast.

Instructions on page 65

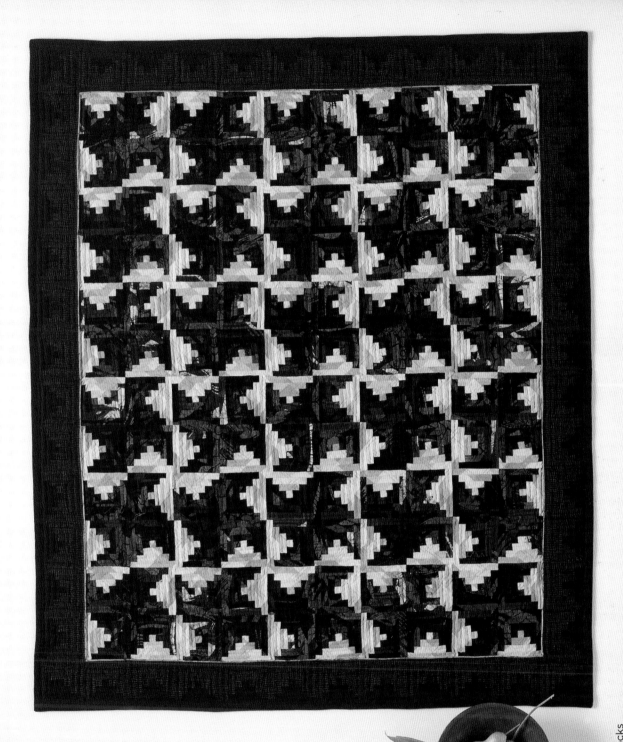

WINDMILL MINI QUILT

Four identical courthouse steps blocks are pieced together to create this bold windmill motif. The combination of beige check and summerweight cotton kimono fabric in shades of indigo, brown, and black creates a striking contrast and lends an air of movement to the design.

Instructions on page 68

Part One: Basic Log Cabin Blocks

31

Method A: Hand Piece

With this basic log cabin method, you'll hand sew the pieces together starting from the center and working outward in a clockwise direction. Refer to pages 10-13 for hand sewing tips.

Note: In the following example, all pieces are ³⁄₄" (2 cm) wide without seam allowance. This means that the pieces will be 1¹⁄₄" (3.2 cm) wide once seam allowance has been added.

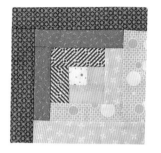
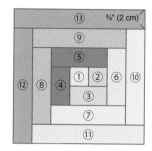

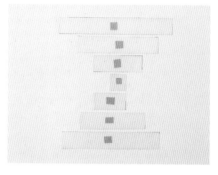

1. Draw a traditional log cabin block following the instructions on page 8. Transfer the pattern onto tracing paper or a mylar sheet to make templates for each pattern piece. Remember, you only need one template for identically shaped pieces. Adhere small pieces of sandpaper to the templates, as shown on page 10.

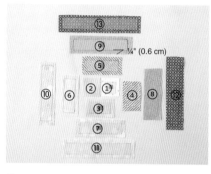

2. Arrange the templates on the wrong side of selected fabrics and cut out each piece, adding ¼" (0.6 cm) seam allowance around each template.

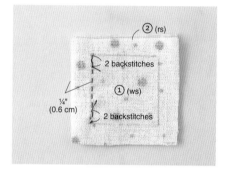

3. Align pieces ① and ② with right sides together. Make two back-stitches starting ¼" (0.6 cm) from the edge. Stitch to the other corner, stopping ¼" (0.6 cm) from the edge and ending the seam with two backstitches.

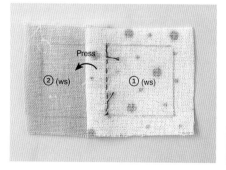

4. Finger press the seam allowance towards the outside. This will be the center section of the block.

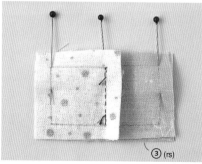

5. Align the center section and piece ③ with right sides together and pin.

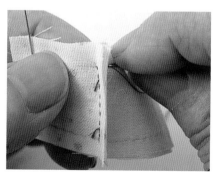

6. Repeat step 3 to attach piece ③ to the center section.

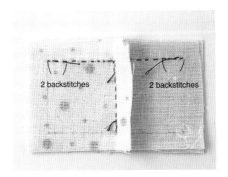

7. Make sure to start and stop sewing at the seam allowances.

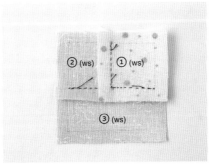

8. Finger press the seam allowance towards the outside.

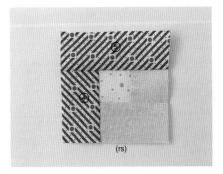

9. Follow the same process to attach pieces ④ and ⑤. The first section of the block is now complete.

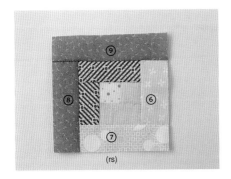

10. Follow the same process to attach pieces ⑥-⑨. The second section of the block is now complete.

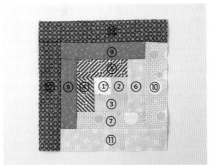

11. Follow the same process to attach pieces ⑩-⑬. The log cabin block is now complete.

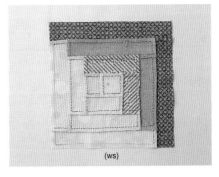

Completed view of the hand pieced block from the wrong side.

Method B: Machine Stitch

The log cabin block is an easy motif to machine stitch because it is composed entirely of straight pieces. As a result, you can use the chain piecing method to construct multiple log cabin blocks at once. For easy piecing without marking the seam allowance, adjust your machine to sew a ¼" (0.6 cm) seam using the edge of your presser foot as a guide.

Note: In the following example, all pieces are ³/₄" (2 cm) wide without seam allowance. This means that the pieces will be 1¼" (3.2 cm) wide once seam allowance has been added.

To avoid tangling your threads when chain piecing, start by sewing through a small scrap of fabric (shown in blue). Sew off the edge of the scrap, then start sewing your first block. A stiletto is useful to guide small pieces under the presser foot.

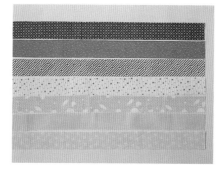

1. Cut strips from seven different fabrics, adding ¼" (0.6 cm) seam allowance to both long edges. Include a contrasting center fabric (shown in white) and three different values of two different colors (shown in blue and yellow).

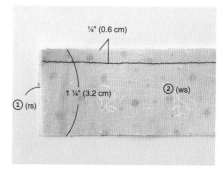

2. With right sides together, sew strips ① and ②, using ¼" (0.6 cm) seam allowance.

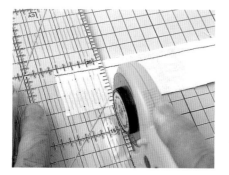

3. Cut a 1¼" (3.2 cm) wide segment from the sewn strip set.

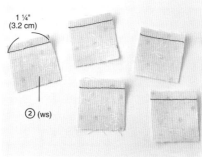

4. Continue cutting the strip set into 1¼" (3.2 cm) wide segments. These will be the center sections of the blocks.

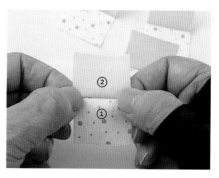

5. Finger press the seam allowance towards the outside.

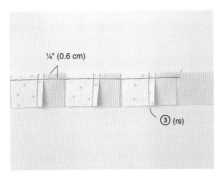

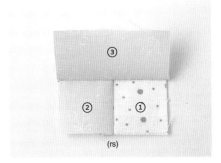

6. With right sides together, align trimmed and pressed center sections with strip ③ (shown in yellow). Pin and stitch using ¼" (0.6 cm) seam allowance.

7. Cut strip ③ into segments to match the center sections.

8. Finger press the seam allowance towards the outside.

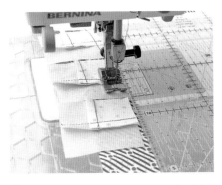

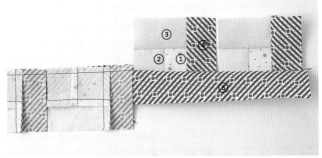

9. Repeat steps 6-8 to attach strip ④ (shown in blue) to the trimmed and pressed units.

10. Follow the same process to attach strip ⑤ (shown in blue). Cut each block apart. The first section of the block is now complete.

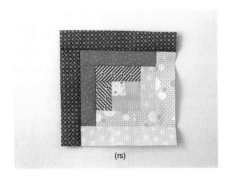

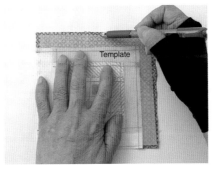

11. Follow the same process to attach strips ⑥– ⑫. The log cabin block is now complete.

12. Use the template to mark ¼" (0.6 cm) seam allowances on all four sides of the block.

This method is ideal for projects that require you to sew multiples of the same block. Rather than sewing one block at a time, you will create four blocks at once!

Method C: Paper Piece

Paper piecing is perfect for making log cabin blocks because it ensures accuracy, even when working on a small scale. With this technique, you won't have to worry about distorting the shape of your pieces during the cutting or sewing processes. Instead, you'll sew your pieces directly onto a foundation paper template complete with guidelines. Simply remove the paper when the block is complete and you'll be left with a perfect block. Shorten your machine's stitch length for ease in removing the foundation paper.

Note: In the following example, all pieces are ³/₄" (2 cm) wide without seam allowance. This means that the pieces will be 1¹/₄" (3.2 cm) wide once seam allowance has been added.

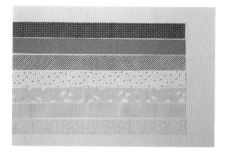

1. Cut strips from seven different fabrics, adding ¹/₄" (0.6 cm) seam allowance to both long edges. Include a contrasting center fabric (shown in white) and three different values of two different colors (shown in blue and yellow).

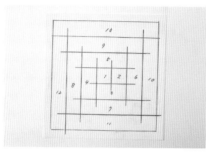

2. Draw a traditional log cabin block following the instructions on page 8. Transfer the pattern onto tracing paper to create the foundation paper template. Make sure to extend the lines at the corners to preserve the right angles.

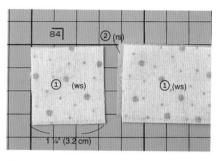

3. Align strips ① and ② with right sides together. Cut into 1¹/₄" (3.2 cm) wide segments.

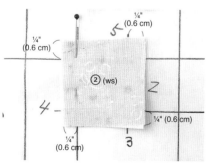

4. Keeping right sides together, position one of the segments on section 1 of the foundation paper template. Pin in place, maintaining an even ¹/₄" (0.6 cm) seam allowance on all sides.

Note: When paper piecing, insert pins next to the line so you'll be able to sew directly on the line with ease.

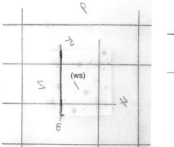

5. Flip the work over so the foundation paper template is facing up. Stitch along the line to sew pieces ① and ② to the foundation paper template.

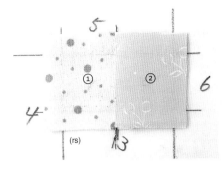
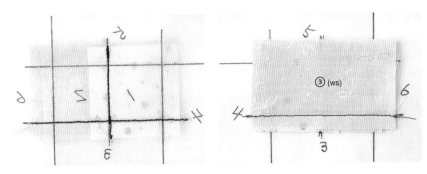

6. Open pieces ① and ②. Finger press the seam allowance to one side. The center section is now complete.

7. Trim strip ③ into a segment equal in size to the center section. Align piece ③ and the center section with right sides together and sew along the line. Make sure you sew with the foundation paper template side facing up.

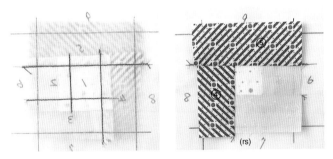
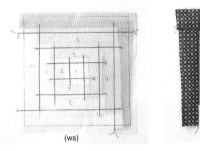

8. Follow the same process to attach pieces ④ and ⑤. The first section of the log cabin block is now complete.

9. Follow the same process to attach pieces ⑥–⑨, then ⑩–⑬. The log cabin block is now complete.

10. Align a ruler next to each line of machine stitching. Use a stiletto to score a line in the foundation paper template.

11. Carefully remove the foundation paper along the scored lines.

This variation on the traditional log cabin block is composed of sections with equally sized pieces. Courthouse steps blocks usually feature a symmetrical arrangement of light and dark colored fabrics. These two elements combine to create a striking visual effect when multiple courthouse steps blocks are pieced together.

Note: *In the following example, all pieces are ³/₄" (2 cm) wide without seam allowance. This means that the pieces will be 1 ¹/₄" (3.2 cm) wide once seam allowance has been added.*

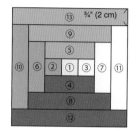

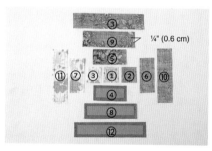

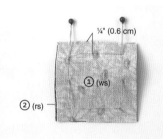

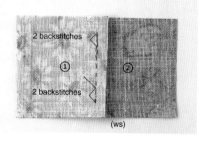

1. Draw a courthouse steps block following instructions on page 8. Transfer onto tracing paper or a mylar sheet to make templates for each pattern piece. Remember, you only need one template for identically shaped block pieces. Arrange the templates on the wrong side of the selected fabrics and cut out each piece, adding ¹/₄" (0.6 cm) seam allowance around each template.

2. Align pieces ① and ② with right sides together and pin.

3. Make two backstitches starting ¹/₄" (0.6 cm) from the corner. Stitch to the other corner, stopping ¹/₄" (0.6 cm) from the edge and ending the seam with two backstitches. Finger press the seam allowance towards the outside. This will be the center section of the block.

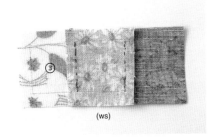

(ws)

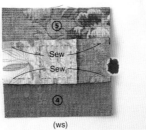

(ws)

(rs)

4. Repeat step 3 to attach piece ③ to the center section.

5. Align pieces ④ and ⑤ along the top and bottom of the section from step 4. Follow the same process used in step 3 to attach. The first section of the block is now complete.

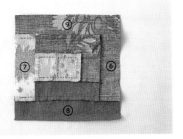

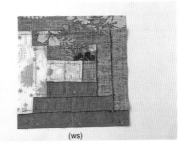

(ws)

(rs)

6. Follow the same process to attach pieces ⑥-⑨. The second section of the block is now complete.

7. Follow the same process to attach pieces ⑩-⑬. The courthouse steps block is now complete.

HOW TO SEW DOUBLE-SIDED LOG CABIN BLOCKS

This innovative technique uses the sewing machine to construct a double-sided block featuring two different log cabin motifs. With this method, everything is made from fabric strips, except for the center sections. Cut strips from two different fabrics, adding ³⁄₈" (1 cm) seam allowance to both long edges. The seam allowance is slightly larger than normal because this technique uses batting.

Note: *In the following example, all pieces are ³⁄₄" (2 cm) wide without seam allowance, unless otherwise noted. This means that the pieces will be 1¹⁄₂" (4 cm) wide once seam allowance has been added.*

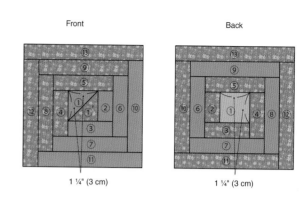

1 ¼" (3 cm)   1 ¼" (3 cm)

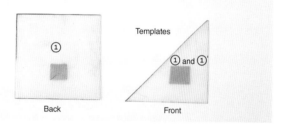

1. Make templates for the center sections of both the front and back blocks.

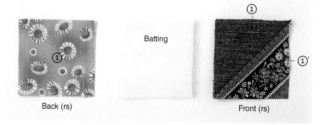

2. Cut out the two pieces for the front center section, adding ³⁄₈" (1 cm) seam allowance. With right sides together, sew the two pieces along the diagonal of the triangle. Cut the back center section out of both fabric and batting, adding ³⁄₈" (1 cm) seam allowance.

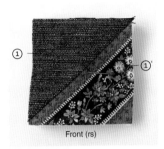

Front (rs)
① ①'

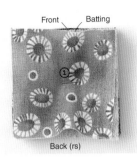

Front   Batting
①
Back (rs)

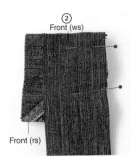

②
Front (ws)
Front (rs)

②
Back (ws)   ① Back (rs)

3. Layer the back center section, batting, and front center section with right sides facing out and pin.

4. Pin the front center section and front strip ② with right sides together.

5. Pin the back center section and back strip ② with right sides together. You should now have five layers pinned together.

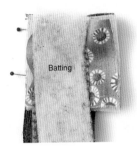

Batting

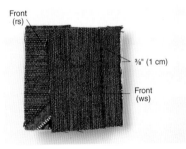

Front (rs)
⅜" (1 cm)
Front (ws)

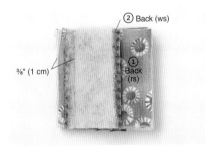

② Back (ws)
① Back (rs)
⅜" (1 cm)

6. Layer a 1½" (4 cm) wide strip of batting on top of back strip ②.

7. Flip the work over so the front is facing you. Sew from edge to edge along the right side using ⅜" (1 cm) seam allowance. Trim the excess fabric and batting strips.

8. Pieces ① and ② are now attached for both the front and back. Turn each piece right side out.

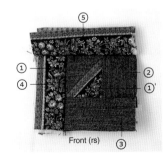

⑤
① ②
④ ①'
Front (rs) ③

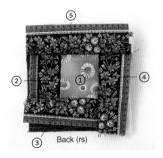

⑤
② ① ④
①
③ Back (rs)

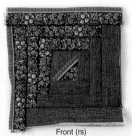

Front (rs)

Back (rs)

9. Repeat steps 4-8 to attach pieces ③-⑤ for both the front and back. The first section of the block is now complete.

10. Follow the same process to complete the second and third sections of the block for both the front and back.

Part One: Basic Log Cabin Blocks

PETITE PIN CUSHIONS

shown on page 22

Finished Size: About 2 ³/₄" x 2 ³/₄" (7 x 7 cm)

Note: *Use mousseline de laine (a lightweight wool fabric) and wool stuffing to prevent pins and needles from rusting. If you can't find wool, it's alright to use cotton fabric and cotton/polyester stuffing.*

RECOMMENDED CONSTRUCTION TECHNIQUE:

Method A: Hand Piece...page 32

Materials

Variation 1
• Scraps of orange floral print and light green solid (for log cabin pieces)
• 4" x 8" (10 x 20 cm) of print (for backing and bottom)

Variation 2
• Scraps of red solid, yellow solid, purple solid, and floral print (for log cabin pieces)
• 4" x 8" (10 x 20 cm) of print (for backing and bottom)

Variation 3
• Scraps of light blue, dark green, and star print (for log cabin pieces)
• 4" x 8" (10 x 20 cm) of purple print (for backing and bottom)

Variation 4
• Scraps of dark brown solid, purple print, and red floral print (for log cabin pieces)
• 4" x 8" (10 x 20 cm) of print (for backing and bottom)

Variation 5
• Scraps of green solid, red print, and orange print (for log cabin pieces)
• 4" x 8" (10 x 20 cm) of green solid (for backing and bottom)

All Variations
• Small amount of stuffing for each pin cushion

Sew using ¼" (0.6 cm) seam allowances, unless otherwise noted.

Construction Steps

1. Cut the log cabin pieces

Create templates for each log cabin piece, as shown on page 10. Cut out each piece for desired design, following dimensions provided in the diagrams. Make sure to add ¼" (0.6 cm) seam allowance when cutting the pieces out of fabric.

Variation 1

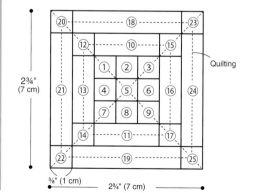

2¾" (7 cm)

³/₈" (1 cm)

2¾" (7 cm)

Quilting

All pieces are ³/₈" (1 cm) wide.

PIECE	FABRIC
① ③ ⑤ ⑦ ⑨ ⑫ ⑭ ⑮ ⑰ ⑳ ㉒ ㉓ ㉕	light green solid
② ④ ⑥ ⑧ ⑩ ⑪ ⑬ ⑯ ⑱ ⑲ ㉑ ㉔	orange floral print

Variation 2

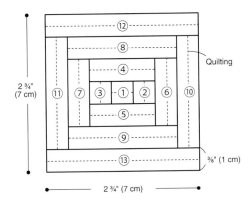

All pieces are ³⁄₈" (1 cm) wide.

PIECE	FABRIC
①	red solid
② ③ ⑥ ⑦ ⑩ ⑪	floral print
④ ⑧ ⑫	purple solid
⑤ ⑨ ⑬	yellow solid

Variation 3

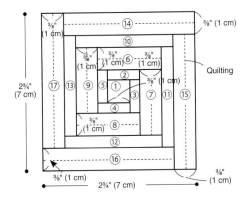

All pieces are ¹⁄₄" (0.5 cm) wide, unless otherwise noted.

PIECE	FABRIC
①	light blue solid
②~⑤ ⑩~⑬	dark green solid
⑥~⑨ ⑭~⑰	star print

Variation 4

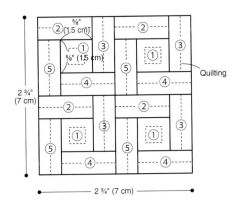

All pieces are ³⁄₈" (1 cm) wide, unless otherwise noted.

PIECE	FABRIC
①	cut 4 of red floral print
②~⑤	cut 1 each of purple print and 3 each of brown solid

Variation 5

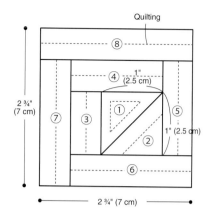

PIECE	FABRIC
①	green solid
②⑤⑥	red print
③④⑦⑧	orange print

2. Make the log cabin block for the top

For variation 1, sew pieces ①-㉕ together in numerical order, as shown in the diagrams below. For variations 2 and 5, sew the pieces together as shown on page 43 and above. For variations 3 and 4, sew pieces ①-⑤ together in numerical order, making sure to inset the seams, as shown in the diagrams below. Sew the four blocks together for variation 4. Trim all seam allowances to ¼" (0.5 cm).

Variation 1

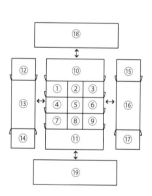

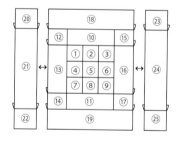

Variations 3 & 4

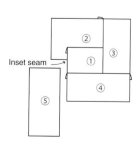

Variation 4

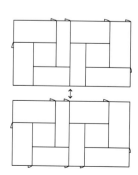

3. Make the backing

Cut out a 3 ½" x 3 ½" (9 x 9 cm) piece for the backing. Layer top and backing. Baste. Cut out another 3 ½" x 3 ½" (9 x 9 cm) piece for the bottom. Note: These measurements include seam allowance.

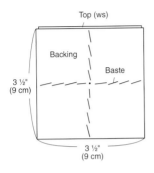

Top (ws)

Backing

Baste

3 ½"
(9 cm)

3 ½"
(9 cm)

4. Quilt

Quilt the log cabin block (batting is not used here to prevent pins and needles from rusting). Use the diagram below for variation 1 and the diagrams on pages 43-44 for variations 2-5.

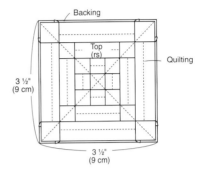

Backing

Top
(rs)

Quilting

3 ½"
(9 cm)

3 ½"
(9 cm)

5. Sew the pin cushion together

Align the top and bottom with right sides together and sew, leaving a 1 ¼" (3 cm) opening. Use ⅜" (1 cm) seam allowance.

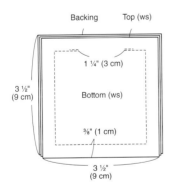

Backing   Top (ws)

1 ¼" (3 cm)

3 ½"
(9 cm)

Bottom (ws)

⅜" (1 cm)

3 ½"
(9 cm)

6. Finish the pin cushion

Trim excess seam allowance to ¼" (0.7 cm) and turn right side out. Stuff the pin cushion with wool, then whipstitch the opening.

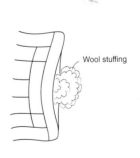

Wool stuffing

DOUBLE DUTY POT HOLDERS

shown on page 23

Finished Size: About 6 ¾" x 6 ¾" (17 x 17 cm)

RECOMMENDED CONSTRUCTION TECHNIQUE:
Double-Sided Log Cabin Block...page 40

Materials

Variation 1

- 59 ¾" (152 cm) of 1 ½" (4 cm) wide strips of blue/green print cotton (for log cabin pieces)
- 2" x 2" (5 x 5 cm) of blue/green print cotton (for center section pieces)
- 1 ½" x 4" (4 x 10 cm) of blue/green print cotton (for loop)
- One 1 ½" x 25 ½" (4 x 65 cm) bias strip of blue/green print cotton (for binding)
- 65" (165 cm) of 1 ½" (4 cm) wide strips of brown print cotton (for log cabin pieces)
- 2" x 4" (5 x 10 cm) of brown print cotton (for center section pieces)

Variation 2

- 39 ½" (100 cm) of 1 ½" (4 cm) wide strips of pink batik cotton (for log cabin pieces)
- 2" x 2" (5 x 5 cm) of pink batik cotton (for center section pieces)
- 53 ⅛" (135 cm) of 1 ½" (4 cm) wide strips of blue batik cotton (for log cabin pieces)
- One 1 ½" x 25 ½" (4 x 65 cm) bias strip of blue batik cotton (for binding)
- 15 ¾" (40 cm) of 1 ½" (4 cm) wide strips of beige print cotton (for log cabin pieces)
- 11 ¾" (30 cm) of 1 ½" (4 cm) wide strips of purple print cotton (for log cabin pieces)

Variation 3

- 55" (140 cm) of 1 ½" (4 cm) wide strips of light purple batik cotton (for log cabin pieces)
- 2" x 3 ⅛" (5 x 8 cm) of light purple batik cotton (for center section pieces)
- 49 ¼" (125 cm) of 1 ½" (4 cm) wide strips of dark purple batik cotton (for log cabin pieces)
- 2" x 3 ⅛" (5 x 8 cm) of dark purple batik cotton (for center section pieces)
- 1 ½" x 4" (4 x 10 cm) of dark purple floral print cotton (for loop)
- One 1 ½" x 25 ½" (4 x 65 cm) bias strip of dark purple floral print cotton (for binding)

Sew using ⅜" (1 cm) seam allowances, unless otherwise noted.

Construction Steps

1. Cut the log cabin pieces

Make templates for the center sections of both the front and back blocks. Cut out the pieces, adding ⅜" (1 cm) seam allowance. For each pot holder, cut one 1 ¼" x 1 ¼" (3 x 3 cm) center section out of batting, adding ⅜" (1 cm) seam allowance. Cut out strips for the remaining log cabin block pieces. All strips should be ¾" (2 cm) wide without seam allowance. This means that the pieces will be 1 ½" (4 cm) wide once seam allowance has been added.

Variation 1

Front

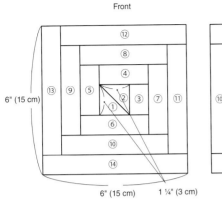

Back

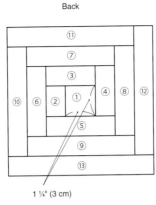

6" (15 cm)

6" (15 cm)   1 ¼" (3 cm)

1 ¼" (3 cm)

All pieces are ¾" (2 cm) wide,
unless otherwise noted.

SIDE	PIECE	FABRIC
Front	①③④⑦⑧⑪⑫	blue/green print
Front	②⑤⑥⑨⑩⑬⑭	brown print
Back	①⑥〜⑨	brown print
Back	②〜⑤、⑩〜⑬	blue/green print

Variation 2

Front

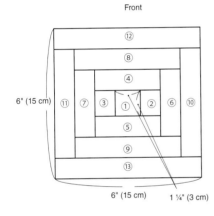

Back

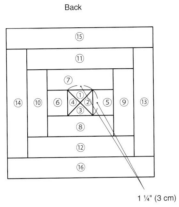

6" (15 cm)

6" (15 cm)   1 ¼" (3 cm)

1 ¼" (3 cm)

All pieces are ¾" (2 cm) wide,
unless otherwise noted.

SIDE	PIECE	FABRIC
Front	①⑥〜⑨	pink batik
Front	②〜⑤、⑩〜⑬	blue batik
Back	①⑦⑪⑮	beige print
Back	②⑤⑨⑬	pink batik
Back	④⑥⑩⑭	purple print
Back	③⑧⑫⑯	blue batik

Variation 3

Front

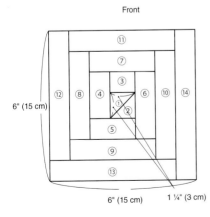

Back

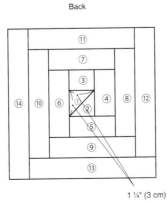

6" (15 cm)

6" (15 cm)   1 ¼" (3 cm)

1 ¼" (3 cm)

All pieces are ¾" (2 cm) wide,
unless otherwise noted.

SIDE	PIECE	FABRIC
Front	①⑤⑥⑨⑩⑬⑭	light purple batik
Front	②③④⑦⑧⑪⑫	dark purple batik
Back	①④⑤⑦⑩⑫⑬	light purple batik
Back	②③⑥⑧⑨⑪⑭	dark purple batik

2. Sew the center sections of the block

For blocks with center sections composed of two triangles, align pieces ① and ② with right sides together and sew along the diagonal. For blocks with center sections composed of four triangles, first sew pieces ① and ② together and pieces ③ and ④ together, then sew the two sets together along the diagonal. Layer the front center section, batting, and back center section with right sides facing out and pin.

Variation 1

Back

Batting

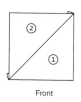

Front

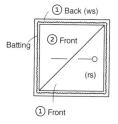

3. Pin

Pin the front center section and front strip ② with right sides together. Pin a 1 ½" (4 cm) wide strip of batting to the wrong side of strip ②. Flip the work over and pin the back center section to back strip ② with right sides together. You should now have six layers pinned together.

4. Sew

Sew from edge to edge along the right side using ³⁄₈" (1 cm) seam allowance. Trim the excess fabric and batting strips, then turn each piece right side out. Follow the same process to attach the remaining log cabin pieces, constructing the front and back simultaneously.

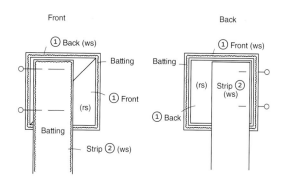

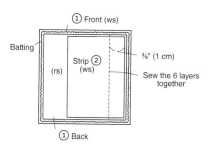

5. Make the loop (variations 1 and 3 only)

Fold each long edge of the loop piece ³⁄₈" (1 cm) and press. Fold the loop piece in half widthwise and topstitch using ¹⁄₁₆" (0.2 cm) seam allowance. Form the piece into a loop and sew to one of the corners on the back of the pot holder.

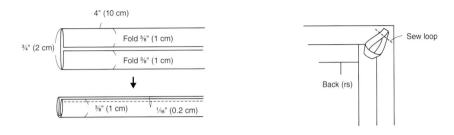

6. Finish the pot holders

Bind the pot holders using the rounded corner binding technique shown on pages 16-17.

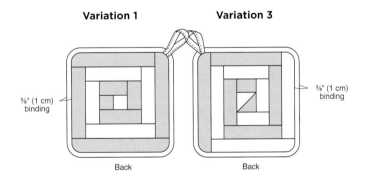

BIAS BLOCK POUCHES

shown on page 24

Finished Size: 5 ¾" (14.5 cm) tall x 7 ⅞" (20.1 cm) wide x 1 ½" (4 cm) deep

Pouch template is located on Pattern Sheet A.

RECOMMENDED CONSTRUCTION TECHNIQUE:

Method C:
Paper Piece...page 36

Materials

Variation 1

• Scraps of beige print and gray solid cotton (for log cabin pieces)
• Two 1 ⅜" x 15 ¾" (3.5 x 40 cm) bias strips of gray solid cotton (for binding)
• 8 ¾" x 12 ⅝" (22 x 32 cm) of brown print cotton (for lining)
• 8 ¾" x 12 ⅝" (22 x 32 cm) of gray solid cotton (for backing)
• 8 ¾" x 12 ⅝" (22 x 32 cm) of batting
• One 7"-9" (18-23 cm) long beige zipper

Variation 2

• Scraps of indigo print and indigo solid cotton (for log cabin pieces)
• Two 1 ⅜" x 15 ¾" (3.5 x 40 cm) bias strips of indigo solid cotton (for binding)
• 8 ¾" x 12 ⅝" (22 x 32 cm) of navy blue check cotton (for lining)
• 8 ¾" x 12 ⅝" (22 x 32 cm) of gray solid cotton (for backing)
• 8 ¾" x 12 ⅝" (22 x 32 cm) of batting
• One 7"-9" (18-23 cm) long navy zipper

Sew using ¼" (0.6 cm) seam allowances, unless otherwise noted.

Construction Steps

1. Make the log cabin block

Cut out strips for the log cabin block pieces. All strips should be ⅜" (1 cm) wide without seam allowance. This means the pieces will be ⅞" (2.2 cm) wide once the seam allowance has been added. Sew the pieces together in numerical order to make the log cabin block. Note: Variations 1 and 2 use the same size block.

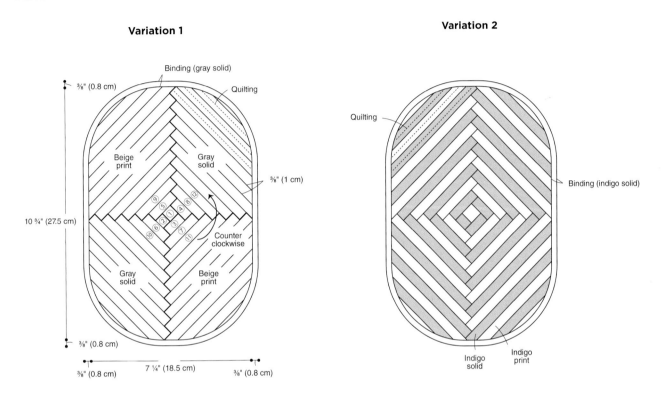

Variation 1

Binding (gray solid)
Quilting
⅜" (0.8 cm)
Beige print
Gray solid
⅜" (1 cm)
10 ¾" (27.5 cm)
Counter clockwise
Gray solid
Beige print
⅜" (0.8 cm)
⅜" (0.8 cm)
7 ¼" (18.5 cm)
⅜" (0.8 cm)

Variation 2

Quilting
Binding (indigo solid)
Indigo solid
Indigo print

2. Quilt and trim the block

Layer the block, batting, and backing. Baste, then quilt as shown in the diagram at right. Use the template on Pattern Sheet A to mark the finishing lines and notches. Trim into shape, leaving ⅜" (0.8 cm) seam allowance.

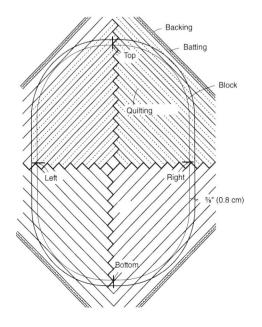

Backing
Batting
Top
Block
Quilting
Left
Right
⅜" (0.8 cm)
Bottom

3. Attach the bias strips

With right sides together, align the center of a bias strip with the top notch and pin. Starting at the center and working outwards, pin the bias strip to each side of the block. Stretch the bias strip slightly along the curve. Sew from each side to the center using ⅜" (0.8 cm) seam allowance. Repeat for the other half of the block.

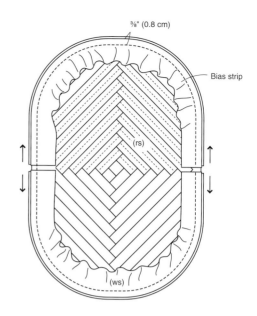

4. Sew the binding

Wrap the bias strips around the seam allowance. Leave the raw edges of the bias strips visible on the wrong side of the block. Stitch in the ditch on the right side to secure the bias strips. Align the center of the zipper with the top notch and pin.

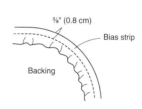

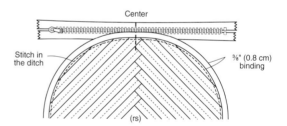

5. Attach the zipper

Starting at the center and working outwards, pin the zipper to each side of the block. To attach the zipper, backstitch from the center to each side. Use the seam from step 4 as a guide when backstitching. Repeat to sew the zipper to the other half of the block.

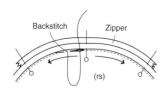

How to Backstitch

6. Sew the pouch together

With right sides together, align the two halves of the block below the zipper. Whipstitch together on each side.

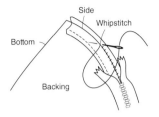

7. Miter the corners

For each corner, match the side seam with the bottom and sew a 1 ½" (4 cm) long seam across the point. Trim the seam allowance to ¼" (0.5 cm).

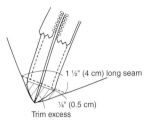

8. Make the lining

Use the pouch template to cut out a lining. Do not add seam allowance. Fold the lining in half with right sides together. Using ¼" (0.5 cm) seam allowance, sew each side together below the zipper position. Repeat step 7 to miter each corner. Attach the lining to the pouch by sewing the mitered corner seam allowances together.

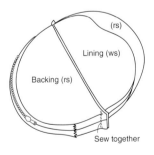

9. Finish the pouch

Fold the raw edge under on the lining and whipstitch to the zipper on the inside of the pouch.

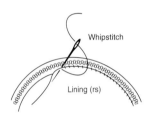

DRAWSTRING CUBE BAGS

shown on page 25

Finished Size: 3 ½" x 3 ½" x 3 ½" (9 x 9 x 9 cm)

RECOMMENDED CONSTRUCTION TECHNIQUE:

Method A:
Hand Piece...page 32

Materials

Variation 1

- 9 ½" x 9 ½" (24 x 24 cm) each of light green, green, and beige solid cotton (for log cabin pieces)
- 6" x 6" (15 x 15 cm) each of yellow, red, purple, and blue solid cotton (for log cabin pieces and loops)
- Two 1 ½" x 17 ¾" (3 x 45 cm) bias strips of purple solid cotton (for drawstrings)
- 2" x 2" (5 x 5 cm) each of red and blue solid cotton (for drawstring charms)
- 13" x 13" (33 x 33 cm) of multicolor print cotton (for lining)
- 8 ¾" x 13" (22 x 33 cm) of any cotton fabric (for backing)
- 4 ¾" x 23 ⅝" (12 x 60 cm) of batting
- Six 17 ¾" (45 cm) long pieces of medium-weight yarn
- Cotton/polyester stuffing

Variation 2

- 9 ¾" x 13 ¾" (25 x 35 cm) of beige solid cotton (for log cabin pieces)
- 6" x 6" (15 x 15 cm) each of light green, red, mustard yellow, and blue solid cotton (for log cabin pieces and loops)
- Two 1 ½" x 17 ¾" (3 x 45 cm) bias strips of green solid cotton (for drawstrings)
- 2" x 2" (5 x 5 cm) each of light green and mustard yellow solid cotton (for drawstring charms)
- 13" x 13" (33 x 33 cm) of multicolor print cotton (for lining)
- 8 ¾" x 13" (22 x 33 cm) of any cotton fabric (for backing)
- 4 ¾" x 23 ⅝" (12 x 60 cm) of batting
- Six 17 ¾" (45 cm) long pieces of medium-weight yarn
- Cotton/polyester stuffing

Sew using ¼" (0.6 cm) seam allowances, unless otherwise noted.

Construction Steps

1. Make the log cabin blocks

Cut out strips for the log cabin block pieces. All strips should be ⅜" (1 cm) wide without seam allowance. This means that the pieces will be ⅞" (2.2 cm) wide once the seam allowance has been added. Sew the pieces together in numerical order to make five blocks for each bag variation. Each variation has four multi-colored blocks for the sides and one solid beige bottom.

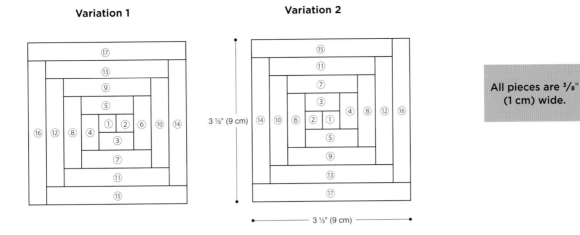

Variation 1

Variation 2

3 ½" (9 cm)

3 ½" (9 cm)

All pieces are ³/₈"
(1 cm) wide.

2. Sew the blocks together

Cut out an equally sized piece of batting and backing for each block. Layer each block, batting, and backing. Baste, then quilt as shown below. With right sides together, sew each side to the bottom, then sew the sides together to create the cube-shaped bag.

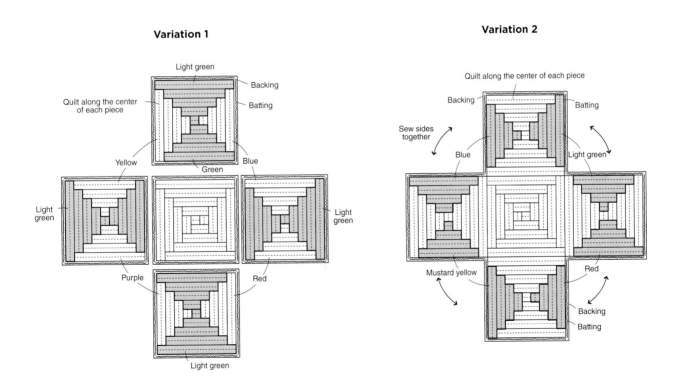

Variation 1

Variation 2

- Unlabeled log cabin pieces are green.
- The bottom block is entirely beige.

3. Make the loops

Cut out a 1" x 2 ½" (2.5 x 6 cm) loop piece from each log cabin fabric (this measurement includes seam allowance). Fold each long edge of the loop pieces ⅜" (1 cm) and press. Fold the loop pieces in half widthwise and topstitch using 1/16" (0.2 cm) seam allowance. Form each piece into a loop, overlapping the ends in opposite directions for every other loop. Baste the loops to the inside of the bag opening at the center on each side.

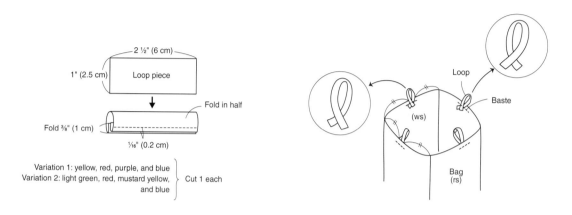

4. Make the lining

Cut out the lining following dimensions provided below. Sew the sides together to create a cube shaped lining. Press the bag opening seam allowances in on both the bag and lining. Insert the lining into the bag and topstitch around the opening using 1/16" (0.2 cm) seam allowance.

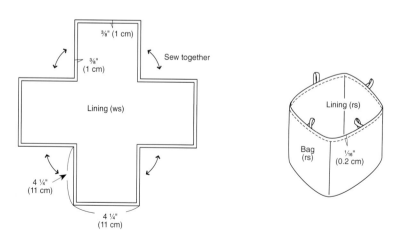

5. Make the drawstrings

Fold each bias strip in half widthwise and sew using ³/₈" (0.75 cm) seam allowance. Use a loop turner to turn each bias strip right side out and simultaneously insert three strands of yarn. Thread each drawstring through the four loops on the bag.

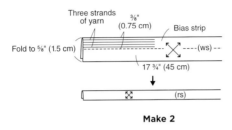

Make 2

6. Make the drawstring charms

Cut out a 2" (5 cm) diameter circle from each drawstring charm fabric. Running stitch each circle using ¼" (0.5 cm) seam allowance. Layer a bit of stuffing on each circle, then pull the thread tail to gather the fabric around the stuffing. Insert the two ends of each drawstring into the stuffing and sew to secure.

Variation 1

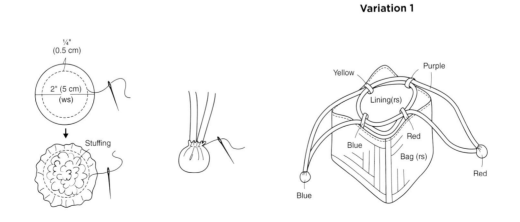

KIMONO BEDSPREAD

shown on page 26

Finished Size: 67" x 89" (170 x 226 cm)

Quilting template is located on Pattern Sheet B.

Note: *The log cabin blocks in this quilt were constructed from silk kimono cloth. The kimono cloth can be substituted for regular silk or traditional quilting cotton.*

RECOMMENDED CONSTRUCTION TECHNIQUE:

Method B: Machine Stitch...page 34

Materials

- 11 ³/₄" x 433" (30 x 1100 cm) of terracotta solid silk (for log cabin pieces)
- 11 ³/₄" x 196 ⁷/₈" (30 x 500 cm) of dark brown print silk (for log cabin pieces)
- 11 ³/₄" x 90 ¹/₂" (30 x 230 cm) of beige solid silk (for log cabin pieces)
- Scraps of 7 different blue and green print and solid silks (for log cabin pieces)

- Scraps of 17 different red and orange print silks (for log cabin pieces)
- 322 ⁷/₈" (820 cm) of 1 ³/₈" (3.5 cm) wide bias strips of dark brown print silk (for binding)
- 72 ¹/₈" x 94 ¹/₈" (183 x 239 cm) of cotton print (for backing)
- 72 ¹/₈" x 94 ¹/₈" (183 x 239 cm) of batting

Sew using ¹/₄" (0.6 cm) seam allowances, unless otherwise noted.

Construction Steps

1. Make the Pattern A blocks

Cut out strips for the log cabin block pieces. All strips should be ³/₄" (2 cm) wide without seam allowance. This means the pieces will be 1 ¹/₄" (3.2 cm) wide once the seam allowance has been added. Sew the pieces together in numerical order to make 52 Pattern A blocks.

Pattern A (make 52)

5 ½" (14 cm)

5 ½" (14 cm)

All strips are ³/₄" (2 cm) wide.

PIECE	FABRIC
①	dark brown print
②~⑬	terracotta solid

2. Make the Pattern B blocks

Follow the same process used in step 1 to cut out strips for the log cabin block pieces. Sew the pieces together in numerical order to make 140 Pattern B blocks. Note: Patterns A and B use the same log cabin block motif and are the same size, but have different fabric layouts. Sew the pattern B blocks together in groups of four, following the order indicated in the diagram at right. This will create 35 large blocks.

Pattern B (make 140)

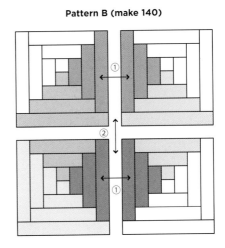

3. Sew the blocks together and quilt

Sew the large Pattern B blocks together in seven rows of five, as shown on page 60. Sew 12 Pattern A blocks together for each of the top and bottom borders. Sew 14 Pattern A blocks together for each of the left and right borders. Sew the borders to the assembled Pattern B blocks to complete the quilt top. Cut the batting and backing so they are 6" (15 cm) larger than the quilt top. Layer the top, batting, and backing. Baste, then quilt as shown in the diagram below (also refer to pages 14-16 for quilting instructions).

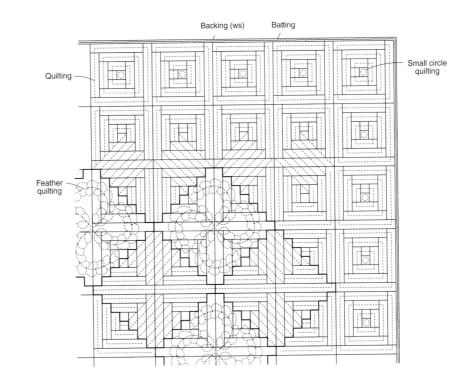

The feather quilting template is located on Pattern Sheet B.

4. Finish the quilt

Follow the instructions on pages 16-20 to bind the quilt.

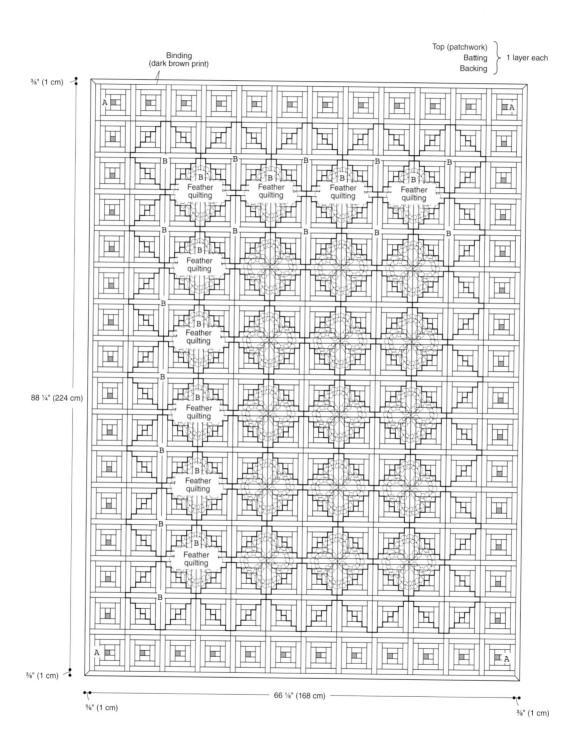

PERFECT PATCHWORK PILLOWS

shown on page 28

Finished Size: 18 ⅞" x 18 ⅞" (48 x 48 cm)

RECOMMENDED CONSTRUCTION TECHNIQUE:

Method B: Machine Stitch...page 34

Materials

Variation 1

- a: 23 ⅝" x 43 ¼" (60 x 110 cm) of beige solid tropical wool (for log cabin pieces, border, and bottom)
- 6" x 13 ¾" (15 x 35 cm) each of ocher (b), terracotta (c), mauve (d), navy blue (e), maroon (f), plum (g), brown (h), and light pink (i) solid mousseline de laine
- 21 ¼" x 21 ¼" (54 x 54 cm) of solid cotton (for backing)
- 21 ¼" x 21 ¼" (54 x 54 cm) of batting

Variation 2

- a: 23 ⅝" x 55" (60 x 140 cm) of beige solid tropical wool (for log cabin pieces, border, and bottom)
- b: 13 ¾" x 17 ¾" (35 x 45 cm) of green solid mousseline de wool (for log cabin pieces)

- c: 8 ¾" x 9 ¾" (22 x 25 cm) of mustard yellow solid mousseline de laine (for log cabin pieces)
- 21 ¼" x 21 ¼" (54 x 54 cm) of solid cotton (for backing)
- 21 ¼" x 21 ¼" (54 x 54 cm) of batting

Variation 3

- a: 23 ⅝" x 37 ½" (60 x 95 cm) of brown and white check cotton (for log cabin pieces and bottom)
- b: 11 ¾" x 23 ⅝" (30 x 60 cm) of indigo solid cotton (for log cabin pieces and borders)
- c: 11 ¾" x 23 ⅝" (30 x 60 cm) of indigo print cotton (for log cabin pieces)
- d: 11 ¾" x 23 ⅝" (30 x 60 cm) of brown solid cotton (for log cabin pieces)
- 21 ¼" x 21 ¼" (54 x 54 cm) of solid cotton (for backing)
- 21 ¼" x 21 ¼" (54 x 54 cm) of batting

Variation 4

- a: 11 ¾" x 43 ¼" (30 x 90 cm) of black print cotton (for log cabin pieces)
- b: 27 ½" x 43 ¼" (70 x 110 cm) of brown and black plaid cotton (for log cabin pieces, border, and bottom)
- 21 ¼" x 21 ¼" (54 x 54 cm) of solid cotton (for backing)
- 21 ¼" x 21 ¼" (54 x 54 cm) of batting

All Variations

- 18" x 18" (45.5 x 45.5 cm) square pillow insert

Sew using ¼" (0.6 cm) seam allowances, unless otherwise noted.

Construction Steps

1. Make the log cabin blocks

Make templates for the center sections of the blocks. Cut out the pieces, adding ¼" (0.6 cm) seam allowance. Cut out strips for the remaining log cabin block pieces. All strips should be ⅝" (1.5 cm) wide without seam allowance. This means the pieces will be 1⅛" (2.7 cm) wide once the seam allowance has been added. For variation 4 only, cut fabric a pieces out on the bias. Sew the pieces together in numerical order, as shown in the diagrams below. Make 8 of each Pattern A and Pattern B blocks for variation 1. Make 16 Pattern A blocks for variations 2, 3, and 4. Note: All variations use the same size log cabin blocks, but have different fabric layouts. Refer to step 2 below and on page 63 for fabric layouts of each variation.

All pieces are ⅝" (1.5 cm) wide, unless otherwise noted.

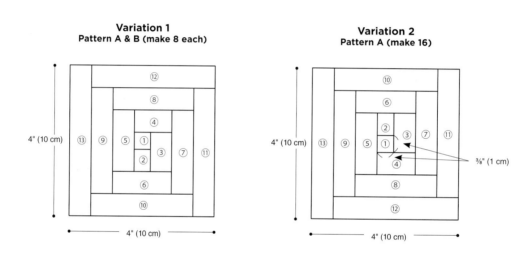

Variation 1
Pattern A & B (make 8 each)

Variation 2
Pattern A (make 16)

2. Sew the blocks together.

Sew the blocks together in four rows of four, according to the diagrams for each variation.

Variation 1

Fabric Layout Diagram

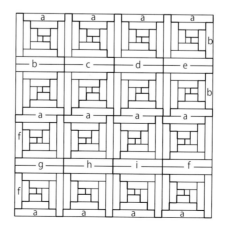

Block Layout Diagram

Variation 2

Fabric Layout Diagram

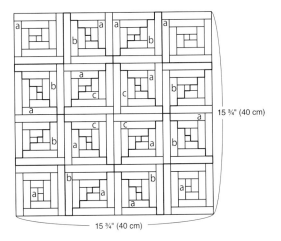

15 ¾" (40 cm)

15 ¾" (40 cm)

Block Layout Diagram

◄	A	◄	▷
∀	◄	A	▷
◄	A	▷	A
∀	▷	∀	A

Variation 3

Fabric Layout Diagram

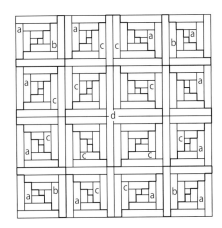

Block Layout Diagram

◄	◄	A	A
◄	◄	A	A
∀	∀	▷	▷
∀	∀	∀	▷

Variation 4

Fabric Layout Diagram

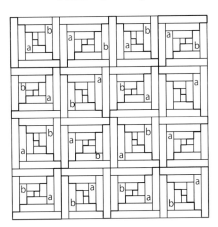

Block Layout Diagram

A	▷	A	▷
◄	∀	◄	∀
A	▷	A	▷
◄	∀	◄	∀

3. Add the borders and quilt

Cut out four 1 ½" x 17 ¼" (4 x 44 cm) border pieces, adding ⅜" (1 cm) seam allowance. Sew the borders to the assembled blocks to complete the top. Layer the top, batting, and backing. Baste, then quilt as shown in the diagram below (also refer to pages 14-16 for quilting instructions).

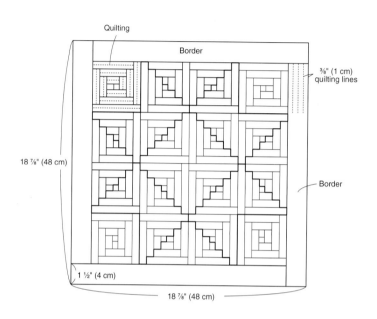

4. Finish the pillow

Cut out a 13 ¾" x 19 ¾" (35 x 50 cm) piece and a 9 ¾" x 19 ¾" (25 x 50 cm) piece for the bottom (these measurements include seam allowance). Zigzag stitch one 19 ¾" (50 cm) long edge on the larger piece. Overlap the two pieces 4" (10 cm) and align with the top with right sides together. Sew the top and bottom together around all four sides using ⅜" (1 cm) seam allowances. Turn right side out and insert a pillow form.

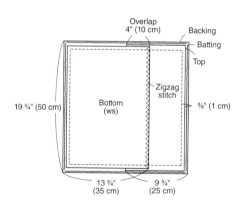

SCARLET TAPESTRY

shown on page 30

Finished Size: 34 ⅝" x 34 ⅝" (88 x 88 cm)

Note: *Pre-wash the cotton cord before making the piping to prevent shrinkage.*

RECOMMENDED CONSTRUCTION TECHNIQUE:

Method B: Machine Stitch...page 34

Materials

- 13 ⅜" x 228 ⅝" (34 x 580 cm) each of red solid cotton in two shades (for log cabin pieces and binding)
- 170 ⅛" (432 cm) of ¾" (2 cm) wide bias strips of cerise solid cotton (for Pattern B block)
- 132 ¼" (336 cm) of ¾" (2 cm) wide bias strips of fuchsia (for Pattern B block)
- 283 ½" (720 cm) of ¾" (2 cm) wide bias strips of magenta solid cotton (for Pattern B block)

- 39 ½" x 43 ¼" (100 x 110 cm) of scarlet solid cotton (for backing)
- 39 ½" x 39 ½" (100 x 100 cm) of batting
- 137 ⅞" (350 cm) of 1" (2.5 cm) wide bias strips of maroon solid cotton (for piping)
- 137 ⅞" (350 cm) of ⅛" (0.3 cm) diameter cotton cord

Sew using ¼" (0.6 cm) seam allowances, unless otherwise noted.

Construction Steps

1. Make the Pattern A blocks

Cut out strips for the log cabin block pieces using one of the red solid fabrics. All strips should be ⅝" (1.5 cm) wide without seam allowance. This means that the pieces will be 1 ⅛" (2.7 cm) wide once the seam allowance has been added. Sew the pieces together in numerical order to make 33 Pattern A blocks.

Pattern A (make 33)

4 ⅛" (10.5 cm)

⑬ ⑨ ⑤ ① ② ⑥ ⑩ ⑫ ⑧ ④ ③ ⑦ ⑪

⅝" (1.5 cm)

4 ⅛" (10.5 cm)

All pieces are ⅝" (1.5 cm) wide.

2. Prepare the bias strips for the Pattern B block

Cut a 2" (5 cm) long and a 2 ¾" (7 cm) long piece from one of the Pattern B block bias strips. Fold each piece in half widthwise with right sides facing out and press. Follow the same process to make a total of four of each size bias strip.

3. Start the Pattern B block

Follow the same process used in step 1 to cut out the log cabin block pieces for the Pattern B blocks using the other red solid fabric. Sew pieces ①-⑤ together in numerical order. Align piece ⑥ with a 2" (5 cm) long folded bias strip sandwiched in between. Make sure the bias strip curves and extends ¼" (0.5 cm) beyond the seam allowance, then sew to attach.

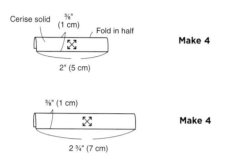

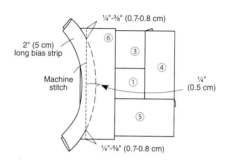

4. Finish the Pattern B block

Follow the same process used in step 3 to attach 2" (5 cm) long bias strips when adding pieces ⑦-⑨ and 2 ¾" (7 cm) long bias strips when adding pieces ⑩-⑬. Note: The bias strips should extend ⅛"-¼" (0.3-0.5 cm beyond the seam allowances for pieces ⑩-⑬. Repeat steps 2-4 to make a total of 31 Pattern B blocks (make 9 with cerise bias strips, 7 with fuchsia bias strips, and 15 with magenta bias strips).

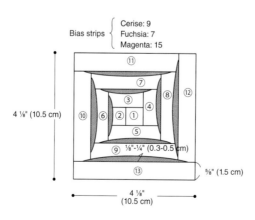

5. Sew the quilt together

Sew the Pattern A and B blocks together, as shown in the diagram below. Distribute the different colored Pattern B blocks evenly throughout the quilt. Cut the batting and backing to 39" x 39" (99 x 99 cm). Layer the top, batting, and backing. Baste, then quilt as shown below (also refer to pages 14-16 for quilting instructions). Follow the instructions on pages 16-20 to make the piping and bind the quilt.

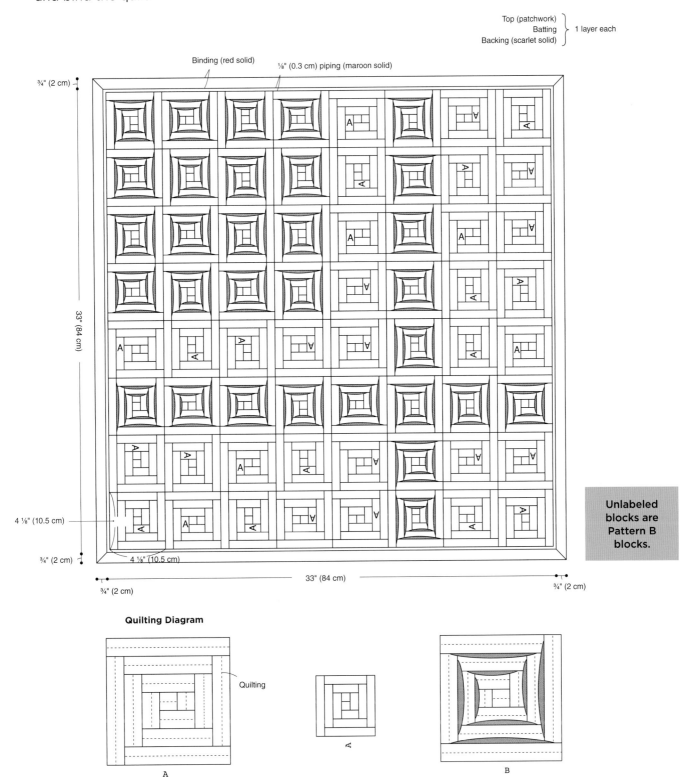

Top (patchwork)
Batting } 1 layer each
Backing (scarlet solid)

Binding (red solid)

⅛" (0.3 cm) piping (maroon solid)

¾" (2 cm)

33" (84 cm)

4 ⅛" (10.5 cm)

¾" (2 cm)

4 ⅛" (10.5 cm)

33" (84 cm)

¾" (2 cm)

¾" (2 cm)

Unlabeled blocks are Pattern B blocks.

Quilting Diagram

Quilting

A

A

B

67

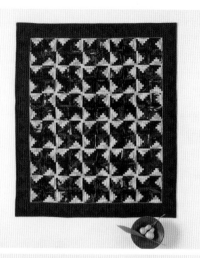

WINDMILL MINI QUILT

shown on page 31

Finished Size: 50 ¾" x 59" (129 x 150 cm)

Notes: *The log cabin blocks in this quilt were constructed from indigo-dyed cotton used for summerweight kimonos. The indigo-dyed cotton can be substituted for any lightweight cotton fabric. Batiks work especially well for this project.*

Pre-wash the cotton cord before making the piping to prevent shrinkage.

RECOMMENDED CONSTRUCTION TECHNIQUE:

Method B: Machine Stitch...page 34

Materials

- 11 ¾" x 31 ½" (30 x 80 cm) of 10 different indigo-dyed print cottons (for log cabin pieces)
- 11 ¾" x 157 ½" (30 x 400 cm) of beige check cotton (for log cabin pieces)
- 11 ¾" x 126" (30 x 320 cm) of brown check cotton (for log cabin pieces)
- 11 ¾" x 102 ⅜" (30 x 260 cm) of brown solid cotton (for log cabin pieces and binding)

- 55 ½" x 63 ¾" (141 x 162 cm) of dark brown print (for backing)
- 55 ½" x 63 ¾" (141 x 162 cm) of batting
- 189" (480 cm) of 1" (2.5 cm) wide bias strips of light brown print cotton (for piping)
- 189" (480 cm) of ⅛" (0.3 cm) diameter cotton cord

Sew using ¼" (0.6 cm) seam allowances, unless otherwise noted.

Construction Steps

1. Make the log cabin blocks

Cut out strips for the log cabin block pieces. All strips should be ⅝" (1.5 cm) wide without seam allowance. This means that the pieces will be 1 ⅛" (2.7 cm) wide once the seam allowance has been added. Sew the pieces together in numerical order to make 120 of Pattern A, 44 of Pattern B, and 2 each of Patterns C and D. Note: All patterns use the same log cabin block motif and are the same size, but have different fabric layouts. Refer to page 69 for the fabric layout of each pattern.

Log Cabin Block Motif
(make 168 total)

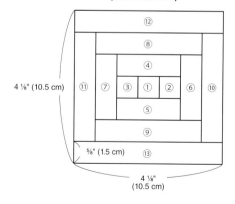

4 ⅛" (10.5 cm)

⅝" (1.5 cm)

4 ⅛" (10.5 cm)

All pieces are ⅝" (1.5 cm) wide.

Pattern A (make 120)

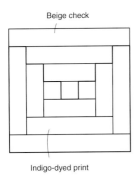

Beige check

Indigo-dyed print

Pattern B (make 44)

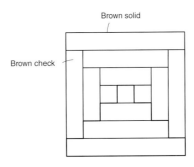

Brown solid

Brown check

Pattern C (make 2)

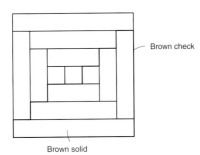

Brown check

Brown solid

Pattern D (make 2)

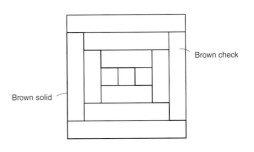

Brown check

Brown solid

2. Make the large A blocks

Sew the Pattern A blocks together in groups of four. This will create 30 large blocks.

Large Block A (make 30)

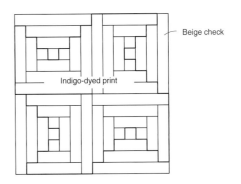

Beige check

Indigo-dyed print

3. Sew the quilt together

Sew the large A blocks together in six rows of five. Follow the instructions on pages 16-20 to make the piping and attach to the assembled large A blocks. To complete the top, attach blocks B-D, following placement indicated in the diagram below. Cut the batting and backing so they are 6" (15 cm) larger than the quilt top. Layer the top, batting, and backing. Baste, then quilt as shown in the diagram below (also refer to pages 14-16 for quilting instructions). Follow the instructions on pages 16-20 to bind the quilt.

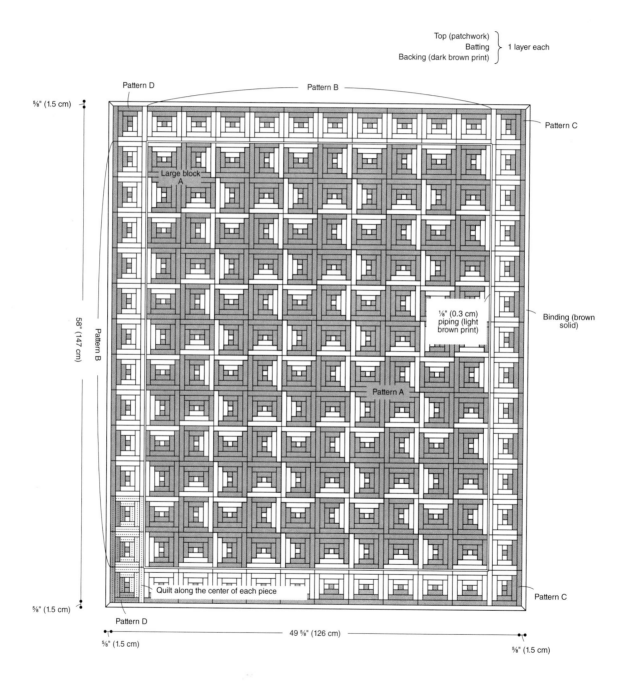

Top (patchwork)
Batting
Backing (dark brown print) } 1 layer each

Pattern D

Pattern B

⅝" (1.5 cm)

Pattern C

Large block A

58" (147 cm)

Pattern B

⅛" (0.3 cm) piping (light brown print)

Binding (brown solid)

Pattern A

Quilt along the center of each piece

Pattern C

⅝" (1.5 cm)

Pattern D

⅝" (1.5 cm)

49 ⅝" (126 cm)

⅝" (1.5 cm)

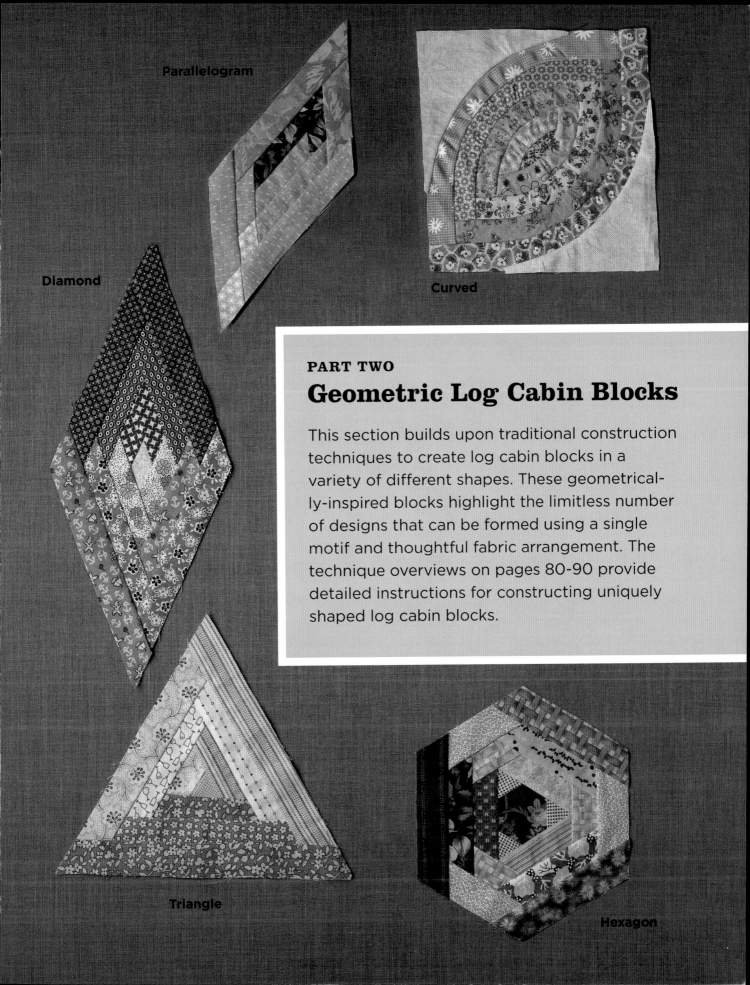

Parallelogram

Curved

Diamond

PART TWO
Geometric Log Cabin Blocks

This section builds upon traditional construction techniques to create log cabin blocks in a variety of different shapes. These geometrically-inspired blocks highlight the limitless number of designs that can be formed using a single motif and thoughtful fabric arrangement. The technique overviews on pages 80-90 provide detailed instructions for constructing uniquely shaped log cabin blocks.

Triangle

Hexagon

TRIANGLE LAP QUILT

This bright and cheerful lap quilt is perfect for those slightly chilly Spring days. Triangle log cabin blocks constructed with light and dark floral prints combine to produce striking circular motifs.

Instructions on page 91

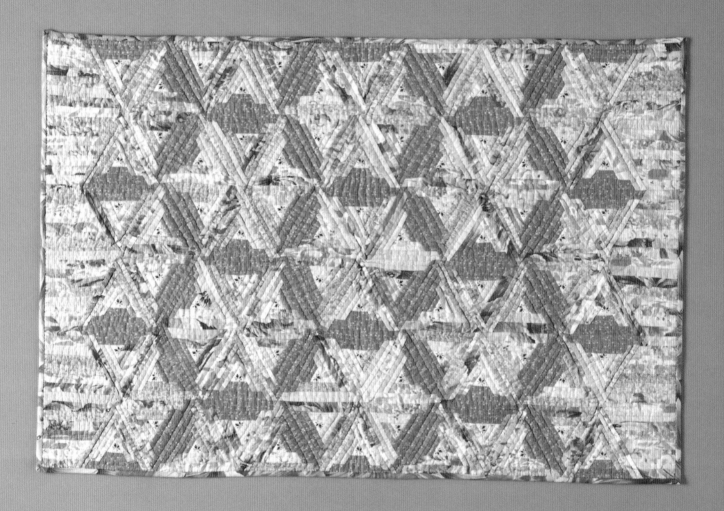

PINK & BLUE STAR TAPESTRIES

Join diamond log cabin blocks together to create the bold eight-pointed stars featured in these tapestries. Use strips in a variety of widths to create the blocks and impart the feel of movement in the Pink Star Tapestry. The Blue Star Tapestry uses small log cabin blocks to create both the star motif and the unique border design.

Instructions on pages 94 and 96

BUTTERFLY TAPESTRY

Showcase the versatility of oval log cabin blocks with these beautiful butterflies. Combine different colors and prints to replicate the uniquely patterned wings. A few well-placed solid oval log cabin blocks give the impression that the butterflies are flying, adding movement to the design.

Instructions on page 99

HEXAGON TAPESTRY

Use the paper piecing technique to sew narrow strips into fun hexagon blocks. Use neutral and indigo fabrics as pictured here, or try brightly colored prints for a kaleidoscopic effect.

Instructions on page 102

1

2

FLOWER TAPESTRIES

Make a basket using a simple hexagon log cab-in block, then fill it with beautifully appliquéd flowers in your favorite colors and patterns. This project uses a variety of techniques to create eye-catching, three-dimensional flower motifs.

Instructions on page 105

PARALLELOGRAM STAR QUILT

Combine traditional log cabin techniques with modern design to create this breathtaking quilted masterpiece. A black background shows off the dynamic starburst designs constructed from parallelogram log cabin blocks.

Instructions on page 110

HOW TO SEW PARALLELOGRAM LOG CABIN BLOCKS

Projects incorporating parallelograms often require symmetrical blocks. Blocks A and A' are constructed using the same process, but feature different fabric layouts, as shown at right.

Note: *In the following example, all pieces are ¹⁄₂" (1.2 cm) wide without seam allowance. This means that the pieces will be 1" (2.4 cm) wide once seam allowance has been added.*

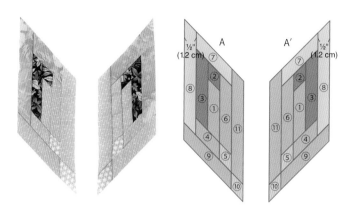

1. Cut strips from four different fabrics, adding ¼" (0.6 cm) seam allowances to both long edges.

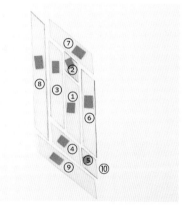

2. Draw a parallelogram log cabin block following the instructions on page 8. Transfer onto tracing paper or a mylar sheet to make templates for each pattern piece. Adhere small pieces of sandpaper to the templates, as shown on page 10.

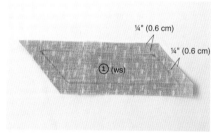

3. Trace the outline of the template onto the wrong side of strip ①. Cut out the fabric, leaving ¼" (0.6 cm) seam allowance around all edges. Follow the same process to cut out all block pieces.

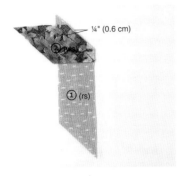

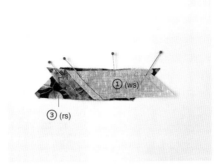

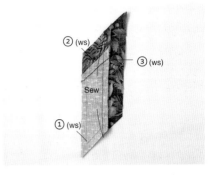

4. Pin pieces ① and ② with right sides together. Sew from edge to edge. Press the seam allowance towards the darker fabric.

5. With right sides together, pin piece ③ to the set from step 4.

6. Sew from edge to edge. Press the seam allowance towards the darker fabric.

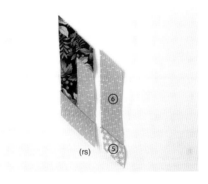

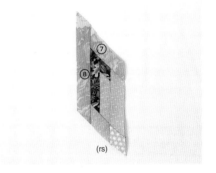

7. Follow the same process to attach piece ④.

8. Align pieces ⑤ and ⑥ with right sides together and sew. Sew this set to the rest of the block.

9. Follow the same process to attach pieces ⑦ and ⑧.

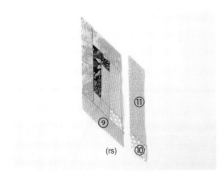

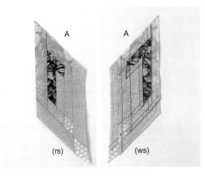

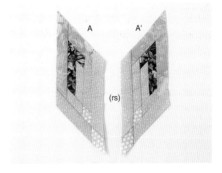

10. Follow the same process to attach pieces ⑨-⑪. Make sure to sew pieces ⑩ and ⑪ together first before attaching to the rest of the block.

11. One parallelogram block is complete.

12. Repeat steps ①-⑪ to complete a symmetrical parallelogram log cabin block. Refer to the diagram at the top of page 80 for fabric layout.

HOW TO SEW DIAMOND LOG CABIN BLOCKS

Diamond log cabin blocks are created by combining straight grain strips with bias cut center pieces. Be careful not to stretch the fabric as you sew, or your diamond will end up crooked.

Note: In the following example, all pieces are ⁵⁄₈″ (1.5 cm) wide without seam allowance. This means the pieces will be 1 ¹⁄₈″ (2.7 cm) wide once seam allowance has been added.

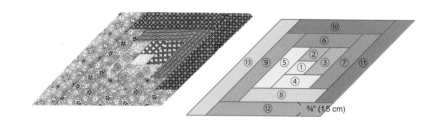

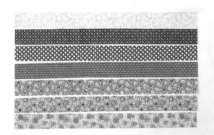

1. Cut strips from seven different fabrics, adding ¼" (0.6 cm) seam allowance to both long edges.

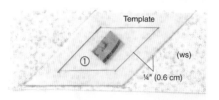

2. Follow the instructions on pages 8 and 10 to draw a diamond log cabin block and make a template of piece ①. Trace the outline of template ① onto the wrong side of strip ①. Cut out the fabric, leaving ¼" (0.6 cm) seam allowance around all edges. Use the same template to cut out piece ②.

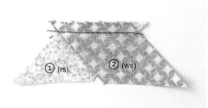

3. Pin pieces ① and ② with right sides together. Sew from edge to edge using ¼" (0.6 cm) seam allowance.

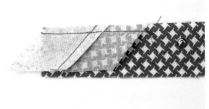

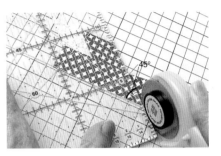

4. Press the seam allowance towards piece ②.

5. Follow the same process to attach strip ③ to the center section from step 4.

6. Open the set from step 5. Using a ruler and a rotary cutter, trim strip ③ at a 45° angle.

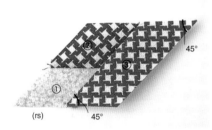

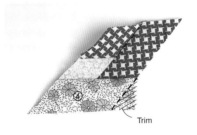

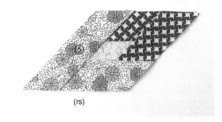

7. Trim the other end of strip ③ into a 45° angle.

8. Follow the same process to attach and trim strip ④.

9. Repeat step 8 to attach and trim strip ⑤. The first section of the block is now complete.

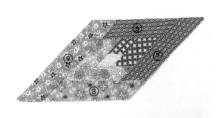

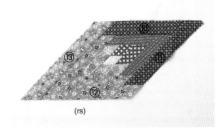

10. Attach pieces ⑥-⑨ to complete the second section of the block.

11. Attach pieces ⑩-⑬ to complete the block.

HOW TO SEW TRIANGLE LOG CABIN BLOCKS

Triangle log cabin blocks are constructed in a similar manner to diamond blocks—each strip is attached, then trimmed into the proper shape before the next strip is added.

Note: *In the following example, each side of piece ① is ⁷⁄₈" (2.3 cm) without seam allowance. This means each side will be 1 ³⁄₈" (3.7 cm) once seam allowance has been added. All other pieces are ⁵⁄₈" (1.5 cm) wide without seam allowance. This means the pieces will be 1 ¹⁄₈" (2.9 cm) wide once seam allowance has been added.*

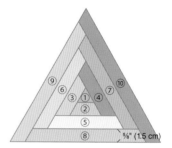

1. Cut strips from seven different fabrics, adding ¼" (0.7 cm) seam allowance to both long edges.

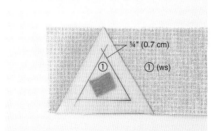

2. Follow the instructions on pages 9 and 10 to draw a triangle log cabin block and make a template for piece ①. Trace the outline of the piece ① template onto the wrong side of strip ①. Cut out the fabric, leaving ¼" (0.7 cm) seam allowance around all edges.

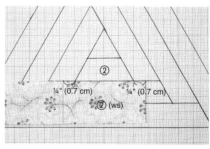

3. Using the pattern as a guide, trim strip ② into shape, adding ¼" (0.7 cm) seam allowance on each side.

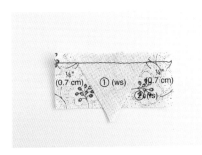

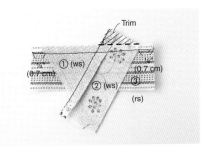

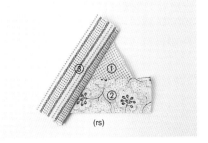

4. Pin pieces ① and ② with right sides together. Sew from edge to edge.

5. Using the set from step 4 as a guide, trim strip ③ into shape, adding ¼" (0.7 cm) seam allowance on each side. Pin with right sides together, then sew to attach. Trim the excess fabric.

6. Completed view of step 5 from the right side.

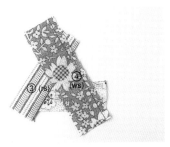

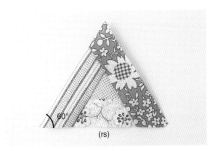

7. Follow the same process to attach piece ④.

8. Using a ruler, trim each corner at a 60° angle. The first section of the block is now complete.

9. Follow the same process to complete the second section of the block.

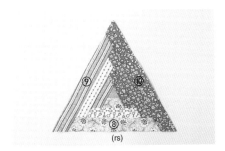

10. Follow the same process to complete the third section of the block.

11. Make a template of the triangle log cabin block. Trace the template to mark the finishing line.

Also known as pineapple motifs, hexagon log cabin blocks can be used to create intricate quilts with a multi-layered appearance. Each block starts off with a small hexagon center piece, then strips are added in traditional log cabin fashion to create a large geometric block.

Note: *In the following example, each side of piece ① is ³/₄" (2 cm) without seam allowance. This means each side will be 1¼" (3.2 cm) once seam allowance has been added. All other pieces are ⁵/₈" (1.7 cm) wide without seam allowance. This means the piece will be 1¹/₈" (2.9 cm) wide once seam allowance has been added.*

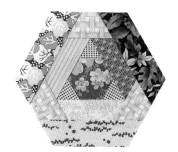
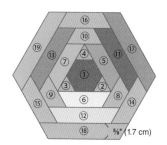

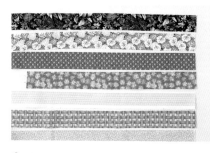

1. Cut strips from seven different fabrics, adding ¼" (0.6 cm) seam allowance to both long edges.

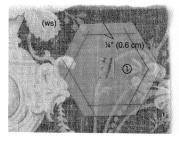

2. Follow the instructions on pages 9 and 10 to draw a hexagon log cabin block and make a template of piece ①. Trace the outline of template ① onto the wrong side of strip ①. Cut out the fabric, leaving ¼" (0.6 cm) seam allowance around all edges.

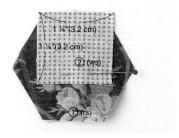

3. Trim strip ② into a 1¼" x 1¼" (3.2 x 3.2 cm) piece. Align pieces ① and ② with right sides together. Insert a pin at the center of the hexagon to hold the two pieces together.

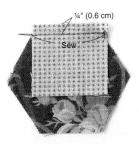

4. Sew from edge to edge, using ¼" (0.6 cm) seam allowance.

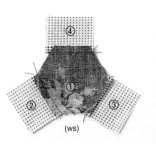

5. Press the seam allowance towards the outside. Follow the same process to attach pieces ③ and ④.

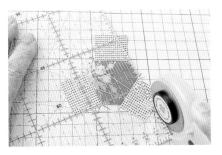

6. Using a ruler, trim pieces ②-④ into triangles with 60° angles.

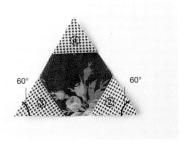

7. The first section of the block is now complete.

8. Trim strips ⑤-⑦ into pieces equal in length to the first section of the block. Align piece ⑥ and the first section of the block with right sides together and sew.

9. Follow the same process to attach pieces ⑤ and ⑦.

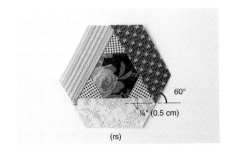

10. Align a ruler ¼" (0.5 cm) below the piece ⑥ seam. Trim the corners of pieces ⑤ and ⑥ at 60° angles. Follow the same process to trim the other corners. The second section of the block is now complete.

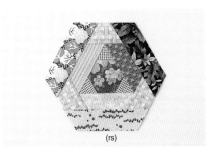

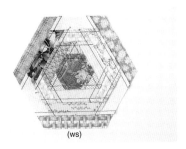

11. Follow the same process to attach the pieces in numerical order and complete the block.

HOW TO SEW CURVED LOG CABIN BLOCKS

The following guide shows how to create curved log cabin blocks using paper piecing. This technique is more challenging than other log cabin blocks because it involves machine sewing along curves. Curved log cabin blocks can also be hand pieced—just make templates and cut out each piece, then hand sew the pieces together.

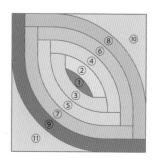

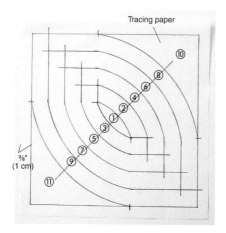

1. Draw a curved log cabin block following the instructions on page 9. Transfer onto tracing paper and add ³⁄₈" (1 cm) seam allowance around the entire block. This will be the foundation paper template.

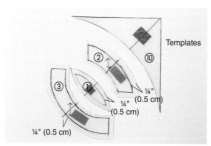

2. Follow the instructions on page 10 to make templates for each piece, adding ¼" (0.5 cm) seam allowance. Do not add seam allowance for piece ⑩.

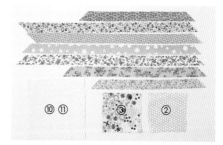

3. Cut out small squares of fabric for pieces ② and ③ and large squares for pieces ⑩ and ⑪. For the remaining pieces, cut strips from seven different fabrics, adding ¼" (0.5 cm) seam allowance to both long edges.

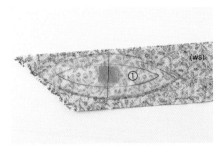

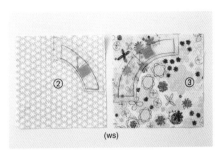

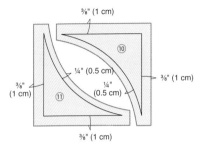

4. Trace the outline of template ① onto the wrong side of strip ①. Cut out the fabric.

5. Position templates ② and ③ on the bias on the wrong side of each fabric. Trace the outlines and cut out the fabric.

6. Cut pieces ⑩ and ⑪ out of fabric, adding ¼" (0.5 cm) seam allowance on the inside curves and ³⁄₈" (1 cm) seam allowance on the outside edges.

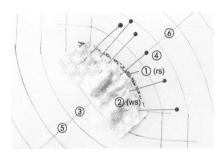

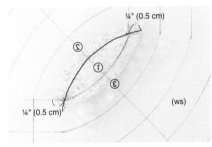

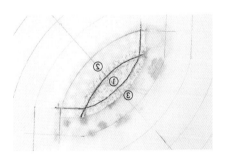

7. Position piece ① on the right side of the foundation paper template. With right sides together, align piece ② on top of piece ① and pin.

8. Flip the work over so the foundation paper template is facing up. Stitch along the line to sew pieces ① and ② to the foundation paper template. Make sure to sew from edge to edge on piece ①.

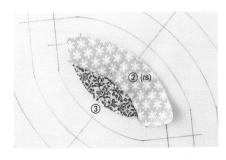

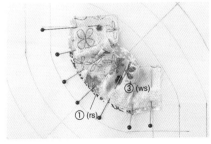

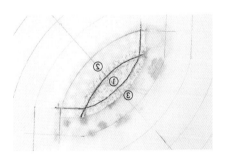

9. Completed view of step 8 from the right side.

10. Follow the same process used in step 7 to pin piece ③ to the center section of the block.

11. With the foundation paper template facing up, stitch along the line to sew pieces ① and ③ to the foundation paper template.

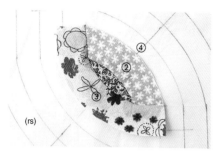

12. Completed view of step 11 from the right side. The first section of the block is now complete.

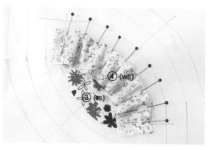

13. With right sides together, pin strip ④ to piece ②. Trim the excess fabric.

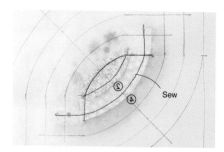

14. With the foundation paper template facing up, stitch along the line to sew pieces ② and ④ to the foundation paper template.

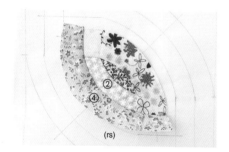

15. Completed view of step 14 from the right side.

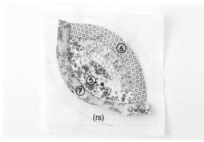

16. Follow the same process to attach piece ⑤ and complete the second section of the block. Attach pieces ⑥ and ⑦ for the third section.

17. Attach pieces ⑧ and ⑨ for the fourth section. With right sides together, align piece ⑩ with piece ⑧. Pin, then sew along the curved line.

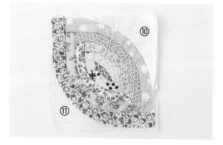

18. Follow the same process to attach piece ⑪. Draw a template of the finished block and trim into shape. Refer to page 37 for instructions on removing the foundation paper.

TRIANGLE LAP QUILT

shown on page 72

Finished Size: 29 ⅛" x 44" (74 x 112 cm)

A full-size template of the triangle log cabin block is located on Pattern Sheet A.

RECOMMENDED CONSTRUCTION TECHNIQUE:

Triangle Log Cabin Block...page 84

Materials

• Scraps of assorted floral print cottons (for log cabin pieces)
• 19 ¾" x 43 ¼" (50 x 110 cm) of pink small floral print cotton (for log cabin pieces)

• 43 ¼" x 49 ¼" (110 x 125 cm) of large floral print cotton (for backing and binding)
• 149 ⅛" (380 cm) of 1 ½" (4 cm) wide bias strips
• 35 ½" x 49 ¼" (90 x 125 cm) of batting

> **Sew using ¼" (0.6 cm) seam allowances, unless otherwise noted.**

Construction Steps

1. Make the log cabin blocks

Make a template for piece ① using the template on Pattern Sheet A. Cut out the fabric, adding ¼" (0.6 cm) seam allowance. Cut out the strips for the remaining log cabin block pieces. All strips should be ⅝" (1.6 cm) wide without seam allowance. This means that the pieces will be 1 ⅛" (2.8 cm) wide once seam allowance has been added. Sew the pieces together in numerical order to make 39 of each Pattern A and B.

Pattern A (make 39)

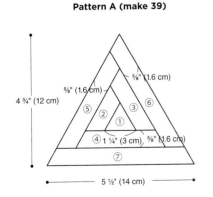

Pattern B (make 39)

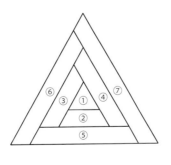

All pieces are ⅝" (1.6 cm) wide, unless otherwise noted.

PIECE	FABRIC
④⑦	pink small floral print
All others	assorted floral prints

PIECE	FABRIC
②⑤	pink small floral print
All others	assorted floral prints

2. Sew the blocks into rows

For Row 1, sew six Pattern A and seven Pattern B blocks together, alternating each block. For Row 2, sew seven Pattern A and six Pattern B blocks together, alternating each block. Make three of each row.

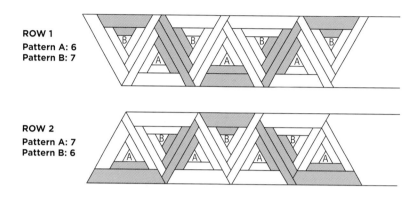

ROW 1
Pattern A: 6
Pattern B: 7

ROW 2
Pattern A: 7
Pattern B: 6

3. Make the Pattern C blocks

Cut out the strips for the Pattern C blocks. All strips should be $^5/_8$" (1.6 cm) wide without seam allowance. This means the pieces will be 1 $^1/_8$" (2.8 cm) wide once seam allowance has been added. Sew 15 strips together, then trim into shape using the dimensions in the diagram at right. Make 6 Pattern C blocks.

**Pattern C
(make 6)**

15 strips (floral prints)

5 $^1/_8$"
(13 cm)

2 $^3/_8$"
(6 cm)

4. Attach the Pattern C blocks to the rows

Sew Rows 1 and 2 together. Sew a Pattern C block to each end. Repeat this process twice more for a total of three sets.

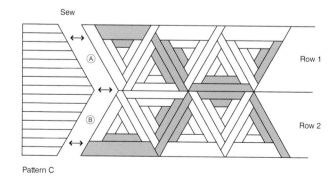

Sew

Ⓐ

Ⓑ

Pattern C

Row 1

Row 2

5. Sew the quilt together

Sew the three sets together to complete the quilt top. Cut the batting and backing so they are 6" (15 cm) larger than the quilt top. Layer the top, batting, and backing. Baste, then quilt along the center of each piece (also refer to pages 14-16 for quilting instructions). Follow the instructions on pages 16-20 to bind the quilt.

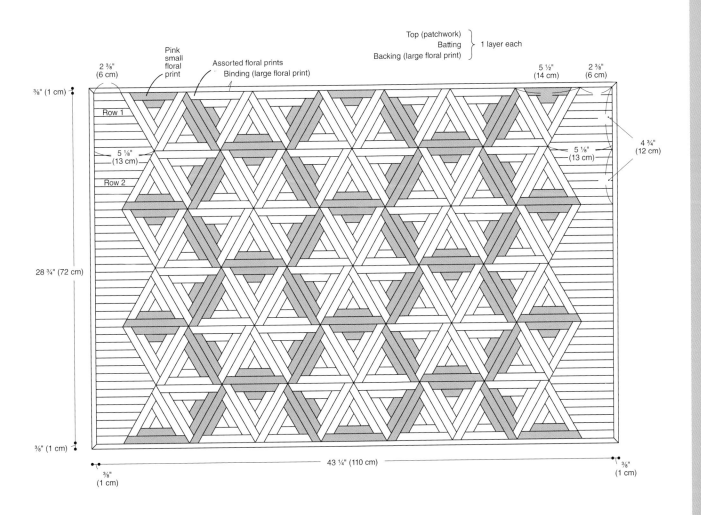

PINK STAR TAPESTRY

shown on page 73

Finished Size: 42 ½" x 42 ½" (108 x 108 cm)

Full-size templates of the diamond log cabin block and the quilting templates are located on Pattern Sheet A.

RECOMMENDED CONSTRUCTION TECHNIQUE:

Diamond Log Cabin Block...page 82

Materials

- 15 ¾" x 19 ¾" (40 x 50 cm) of beige floral print cotton (for log cabin pieces)
- 11 ¾" x 43 ¾" (30 x 110 cm) of pink paisley cotton (for log cabin pieces)
- 9 ¾" x 21 ¾" (25 x 55 cm) of white floral print cotton (for log cabin pieces)
- 43 ¼" x 78 ¾" (110 x 200 cm) of light pink small floral print cotton (for log cabin pieces, pieces c-f and binding)

- 43 ¼" x 43 ¼" (110 x 110 cm) of pink striped cotton (for backing)
- 47 ¼" x 49 ¼" (120 x 125 cm) of batting
- 165 ⅜" (420 cm) of 1" (2.5 cm) wide bias strips of pink solid cotton (for piping)
- 173 ¼" (440 cm) of ⅛" (0.3 cm) diameter cotton cord

Sew using ¼" (0.6 cm) seam allowances, unless otherwise noted.

Construction Steps

1. Make the Pattern A blocks

Make a template for piece ①. Cut out the fabric, adding ¼" (0.6 cm) seam allowance. Cut out the strips for the remaining log cabin blocks. All strips are either ⅜" (1 cm) wide or 1" (2.5 cm) wide without seam allowance. This means that the pieces will be ⅞" (2.2 cm) wide or 1 ⅜" (3.7 cm) wide once seam allowance has been added. Sew the pieces together in numerical order to make 8 of Pattern A. Sew the blocks together to create the star.

Pattern A (make 8)

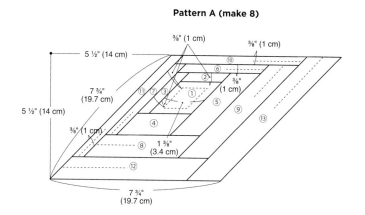

All pieces are 1" (2.5 cm) wide, unless otherwise noted.

PIECE	FABRIC
①④⑤⑫⑬	beige floral print
②③⑥⑦⑩⑪	white floral print
⑧⑨	pink paisley

2. Make the Pattern B blocks

Cut out strips for the log cabin block pieces. All strips should be ⅝" (1.5 cm) wide without seam allowance. This means that the pieces will be 1 ⅛" (2.7 cm) wide once the seam allowance has been added. Sew the pieces together in numerical order to make 44 Pattern B blocks.

Pattern B (make 44)

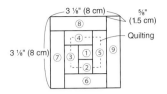

All pieces are ⅝" (1.5 cm) wide, unless otherwise noted.

PIECE	FABRIC
①⑥⑦⑧⑨	light pink small floral print
②③④⑤	pink paisley

3. Sew the quilt together

Cut out four 8 ½" x 8 ½" (21.7 x 21.7 cm) pieces for c and four 6 ¼" (16 cm) high x 11 ¾" (30 cm) long triangles for d. Cut out four 3 ¼" x 29 ⅞" (8.3 x 75.7 cm) pieces for border e and four 2 ¾" x 40 ½" (7 x 103 cm) pieces for border f. Note: These measurements include ⅜" (1 cm) seam allowance. Please sew using this seam allowance. Sew the c and d pieces to the star, then attach a border e piece on each side. Sew the Pattern B blocks together in rows of 11, then sew a row onto each side. Sew a border f piece to each side to complete the quilt top. Cut the batting and backing so they are 6" (15 cm) larger than the quilt top. Layer the top, batting, and backing. Baste, then quilt using the template on Pattern Sheet A. Follow the instructions on pages 16-20 to make the piping and bind the quilt.

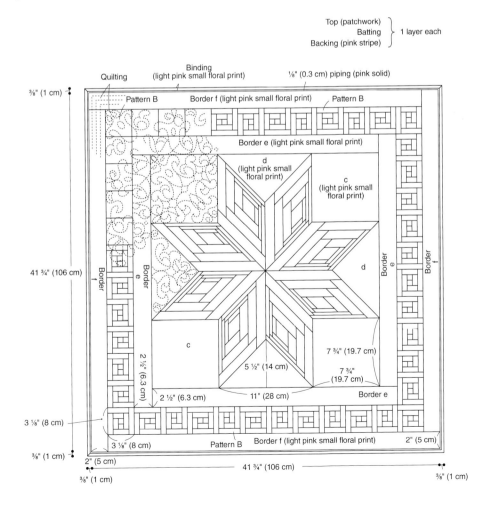

BLUE STAR TAPESTRY

shown on page 73

Finished Size: 38 ½" x 38 ½" (98 x 98 cm)

Full-size templates of the diamond log cabin blocks and the star quilting template are located on Pattern Sheet A.

RECOMMENDED CONSTRUCTION TECHNIQUE:

Diamond Log Cabin Block...page 82

Materials

- Scraps of indigo solid cotton (for log cabin pieces)
- 43 ¼" x 98 ½" (110 x 250 cm) of white and indigo print cotton (for log cabin pieces)
- 43 ¼" x 55" (110 x 140 cm) of white solid cotton (for pieces a-e, borders f and g, and binding)
- 161 ⅜" (410 cm) of 1 ⅜" (3.5 cm) wide bias strips
- 43 ¼" x 43 ¼" (110 x 110 cm) of print cotton (for backing)
- 43 ¼" x 49 ¼" (110 x 125 cm) of batting

Sew using ¼" (0.6 cm) seam allowances, unless otherwise noted.

Construction Steps

1. Make the log cabin blocks

Cut out the strips for the log cabin blocks. All strips are ⅜" (1 cm) wide without seam allowance, unless otherwise noted. This means that these pieces will be ⅞" (2.2 cm) wide once seam allowance has been added. Sew the pieces together in numerical order to make 16 of Pattern A, 16 of Pattern B, and 48 of Pattern C. Note: Templates for the log cabin blocks are located on Pattern Sheet A.

All pieces are ⅜" (1 cm) wide, unless otherwise noted.

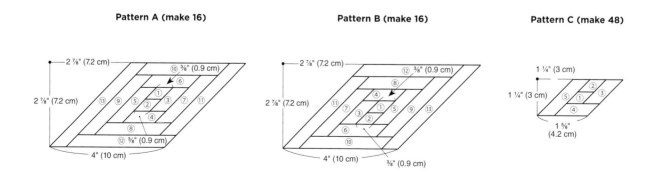

Pattern A (make 16)   Pattern B (make 16)   Pattern C (make 48)

2. Make the large A blocks

Sew two of Pattern A and two of Pattern B together to make a large block A. Make 8 of large block A, then sew together to create the star, as shown on page 98.

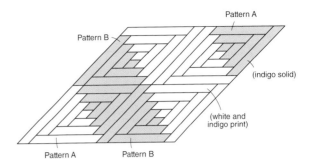

Large Block A (make 8)

Pattern A

Pattern B

(indigo solid)

(white and indigo print)

Pattern A

Pattern B

3. Make the small stars

Cut out pieces d and e, following the measurements included in the diagrams at right. Make sure to add ¼" (0.6 cm) seam allowance to all piece edges. For each star, sew four of piece d to four of Pattern C, then attach one piece e.

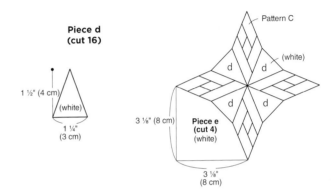

Piece d (cut 16)

1 ½" (4 cm)

(white)

1 ¼" (3 cm)

Pattern C

(white)

d d

d d

3 ⅛" (8 cm)

Piece e (cut 4)
(white)

3 ⅛" (8 cm)

4. Cut out the remaining pieces

Cut out pieces a, b, and c, following the measurements included in the diagrams below. Make sure to add ¼" (0.6 cm) seam allowance to all pieces edges. Cut out the border f and g pieces, following the measurements included in the diagram on the page 98. Make sure to add ⅜" (1 cm) seam allowance to all border piece edges.

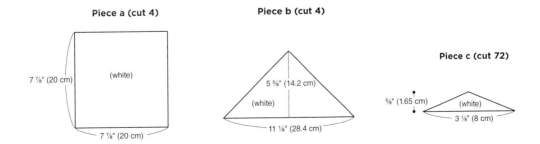

Piece a (cut 4)

7 ⅞" (20 cm)

(white)

7 ⅞" (20 cm)

Piece b (cut 4)

5 ⅝" (14.2 cm)

(white)

11 ⅛" (28.4 cm)

Piece c (cut 72)

⅝" (1.65 cm)

(white)

3 ⅛" (8 cm)

5. Sew the quilt together

Sew the a and b pieces to the star, then attach a border g piece on each side. Sew 18 piece c and 8 Pattern C blocks together. Repeat for a total of four sets. Attach a small star to the end of each set, then sew to border g. Sew a border f piece to each side to complete the quilt top. Cut the batting and backing so they are 6" (15 cm) larger than the quilt top. Layer the top, batting, and backing. Baste, then quilt as shown in the diagram below (also use the star quilting template on Pattern Sheet A). Follow the instructions on pages 16-20 to bind the quilt.

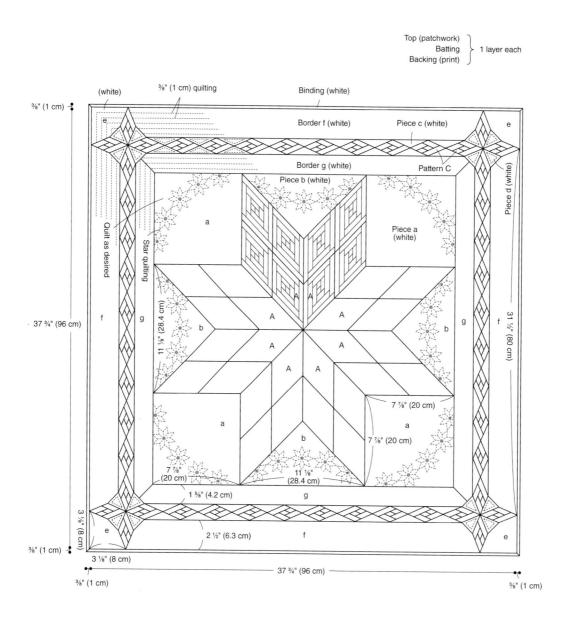

BUTTERFLY TAPESTRY

shown on page 74

Finished Size: 67" x 78" (170 x 198 cm)

Full-size templates of the curved log cabin blocks are located on Pattern Sheet A.

RECOMMENDED CONSTRUCTION TECHNIQUE:

Curved Log Cabin Block...page 88

Materials

- 43 ¼" x 78 ¾" (110 x 200 cm) each of two different dark brown solid cottons (for log cabin pieces and binding)
  - Includes 295 ¼" (750 cm) of 1 ⅜" (3.5 cm) wide bias strips
- Scraps of off-white, khaki, ocher, and brown solids, prints, and stripes (for log cabin pieces)
- 72 ⅛" x 83 ⅛" (183 x 211 cm) of brown print (for backing)
- 72 ⅛" x 83 ⅛" (183 x 211 cm) of batting

Sew using ¼" (0.5 cm) seam allowances, unless otherwise noted.

Construction Steps

1. Make the log cabin blocks

Make templates for pieces ①-③, ⑩, and ⑪ using the template on Pattern Sheet A. Cut out the fabric, adding seam allowance as shown on page 88. Cut out the strips for the log cabin pieces. Without seam allowance, the strips should be ⅝" (1.5 cm), ⅜" (1 cm), or ¼" (0.7 cm) wide. This means the pieces will be 1" (2.5 cm), ¾" (2 cm), or ⅝" (1.7 cm) wide once seam allowance has been added. Sew the pieces together in numerical order to make 28 of Pattern A, 36 of Pattern B, and 8 of Pattern C. Note: Patterns B and C follow the same fabric layout as Pattern A.

Pattern A (make 28)

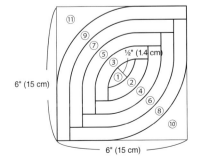

½" (1.4 cm)

6" (15 cm)

6" (15 cm)

All pieces are ⅝" (1.5 cm) wide, unless otherwise noted.

PIECE	FABRIC
①⑩⑪	dark brown solid
③⑤⑦	off-white solid
②	brown print
④	brown and white stripe
⑥	khaki solid
⑧	ocher solid
⑨	brown and white print

Pattern B (make 36)

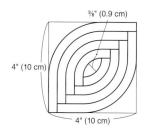

⅜" (0.9 cm)

4" (10 cm)

4" (10 cm)

Pattern C (make 8)

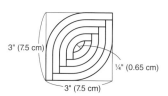

3" (7.5 cm)

¼" (0.65 cm)

3" (7.5 cm)

2. Make Blocks A and B

To make Block A, sew two Pattern A and two Pattern B blocks together. Sew strips to each Pattern B block to complete Block A. Repeat process for a total of eight mixed and three dark brown A blocks. To make Block B, sew two Pattern B and two Pattern C blocks together. Sew strips to each Pattern C block to complete Block B. Repeat process for a total of four B blocks.

Block A (make 8 mixed and 3 dark brown)

Pattern A

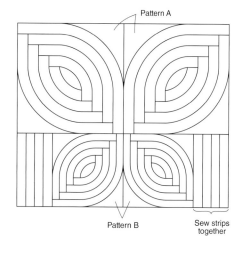

Pattern B

Sew strips together

Block B (make 4)

Pattern B

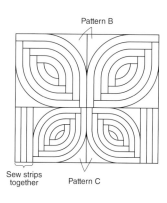

Sew strips together

Pattern C

3. Make the remaining blocks

Sew dark brown strips together to fill in the remaining blocks, as shown in the diagram on page 101. For Pattern D, make a template for piece ①. Cut out the pieces, adding ¼" (0.5 cm) seam allowance. Use the remaining ¾" (2 cm) wide dark brown strips for the log cabin pieces. Sew the pieces together in numerical order to complete the block. Note: The Pattern D blocks vary in size. Therefore, larger blocks may require additional log cabin pieces. Refer to the diagram on page 101 for finished dimensions.

Pattern D

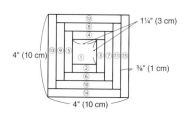

1¼" (3 cm)

4" (10 cm)

⅜" (1 cm)

4" (10 cm)

4. Sew the blocks together to complete the quilt top.

Sew the blocks together to complete the quilt top, following the layout in the diagram below. To make the multi-colored border, sew leftover strips together using ³⁄₈" (1 cm) seam allowance until each piece measures 1 ¼" (3 cm) wide. Sew the border to the assembled quilt top, mitering the corners. Cut the batting and backing so they are 6" (15 cm) larger than the quilt top. Layer the top, batting, and backing. Baste, then quilt as shown in the diagram below. Follow the instructions on pages 16-20 to bind the quilt.

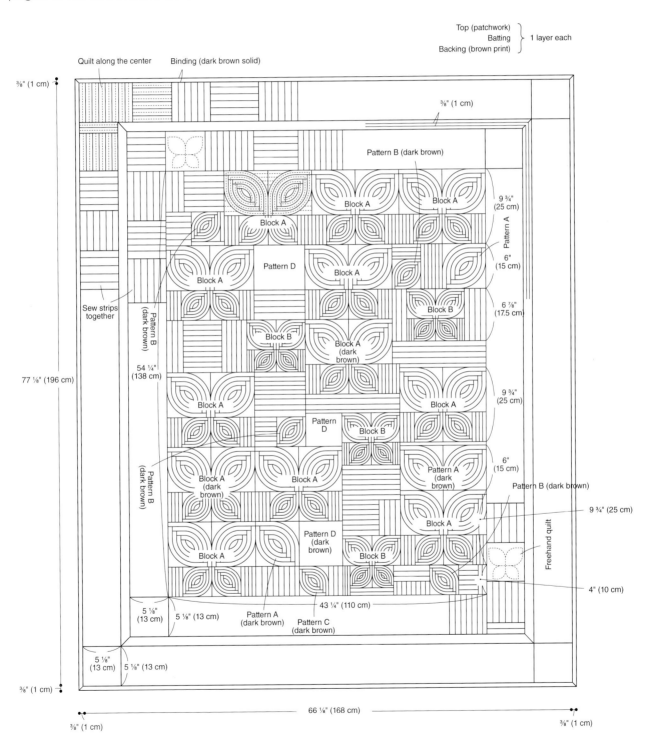

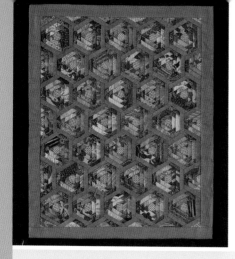

HEXAGON TAPESTRY

shown on page 76

Finished Size: 15 ¾" x 19 ¼" (40 x 49 cm)

Full-size templates of the hexagon log cabin blocks are located on Pattern Sheet A.

Note: *This project is designed without batting or backing because it is meant to be framed. You can always add batting and backing, then finish the quilt following the instructions on pages 14-20.*

Materials

- Scraps of indigo-dyed print, white and indigo small print, and calico print cottons (for log cabin pieces)
- 5 ½" x 35 ½" (14 x 90 cm) of light brown solid cotton (for borders)
- Tracing paper

RECOMMENDED CONSTRUCTION TECHNIQUES:

Hexagon Log Cabin Block...page 86
Paper Piecing...page 36

Sew using ¼" (0.6 cm) seam allowances, unless otherwise noted.

Construction Steps

1. Make the Pattern A blocks

Transfer the Pattern A template on Pattern Sheet A onto tracing paper to create the foundation paper template. Make a template for piece ①. Cut out the fabric for piece ①, adding ¼" (0.6 cm) seam allowance. Cut out strips for the remaining log cabin pieces. All strips should be ⅜" (0.8 cm) wide without seam allowance. This means that the pieces will be ¾" (2 cm) wide once seam allowance has been added. Sew the pieces together in numerical order using the paper piecing construction technique. Make 32 of Pattern A.

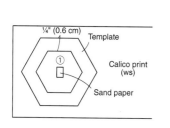

Pattern A (make 32)

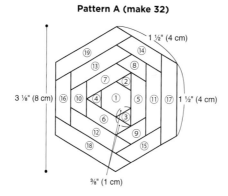

All pieces are ⅜" (0.8 cm) wide, unless otherwise noted.

PIECE	FABRIC
①⑤~⑦ ⑪~⑬	calico print
②~④ ⑧~⑩ ⑭~⑯	indigo-dyed print
⑰~⑲	white and indigo small print

2. Make the other log cabin blocks

Follow the same process to make three of each Patterns B and B', eight of Pattern C, and 2 each of Patterns D and D'. Note: B' is the mirror image of B, and D' is the mirror image of D. Also, piece ① is composed of a strip, so there is no need to make a template for any of these blocks.

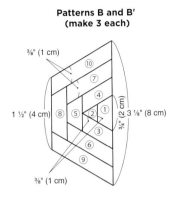

Patterns B and B'
(make 3 each)

⅜" (1 cm)

1 ½" (4 cm)

3 ⅛" (8 cm)

¾" (2 cm)

⅜" (1 cm)

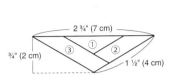

Pattern C
(make 8)

2 ¾" (7 cm)

¾" (2 cm)

1 ½" (4 cm)

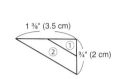

Patterns D and D'
(make 2 each)

1 ⅜" (3.5 cm)

¾" (2 cm)

PIECE	FABRIC
①③④⑥⑦	calico print
②⑤⑧	indigo-dyed print
⑨⑩	white and indigo small print

PIECE	FABRIC
①	calico print
②	indigo-dyed print
③	white and indigo small print

PIECE	FABRIC
①	calico print
②	white and indigo small print

All pieces are ³⁄₈" (0.8 cm) wide, unless otherwise noted.

3. Sew the blocks together

For Row 1, sew five of Pattern A together. For Row 2, sew four of Pattern A together, then attach a Pattern B to one end and a Pattern B' to the other. Repeat for a total of four of Row 1 and three of Row 2. Sew Rows 1 and 2 together alternately, pressing the seam allowances into a Y-shape. Sew the Pattern C, D, and D' blocks to the top and bottom of the assembled quilt top.

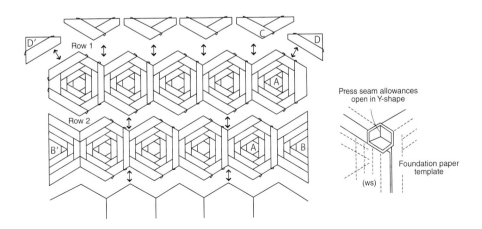

Press seam allowances open in Y-shape

Foundation paper template

(ws)

4. Add the borders

Cut out two border a pieces and two border b pieces. Each border is 2 ¾" (7 cm) wide including seam allowance. Refer to the diagram below for length measurements, making sure to add ⅜" (1 cm) seam allowance to each end. With right sides together, sew each border to the assembled quilt top, then wrap the border around the seam allowance and slip-stitch to the wrong side. Note: The back of this project is not finished because it is designed to be displayed in a frame. As a result, there's no need to remove the foundation paper templates from the wrong side.

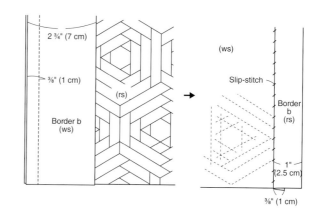

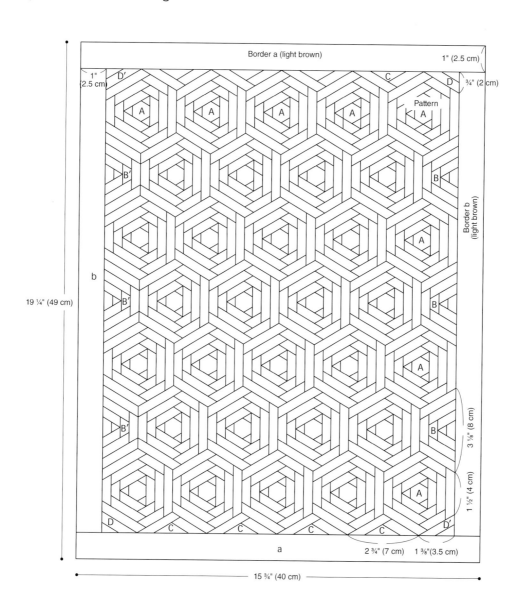

FLOWER TAPESTRIES

shown on page 77

Finished Size: 12 ³/₄" x 13" (32.5 x 33 cm)

A full-size template and applique diagram is located on Pattern Sheet B.

RECOMMENDED CONSTRUCTION TECHNIQUE:

Hexagon Log Cabin Block...page 86

Materials

Variation 1

- 1 ³/₈" x 22" (3.5 x 56 cm) of brown print cotton (for the 1" [2.5 cm] a log cabin pieces)
- ³/₄" x 51 ³/₄" (2 x 130 cm) of brown print cotton (for the ³/₈" [1 cm] a log cabin pieces)
- 15 ³/₄" x 15 ³/₄" (40 x 40 cm) of cream print cotton (for pieces b and c)
- 7 ¹/₂" x 7 ¹/₂" (19 x 19 cm) of pink floral print cotton (for round flower and bud)
- Three 1" x 8 ³/₄" (2.5 x 22 cm) bias strips of light purple print cotton (for six-petal flowers)
- 2 ³/₄" x 4" (7 x 10 cm) of yellow print cotton (for five-petal flowers)
- 4" x 6 ¹/₄" (10 x 16 cm) each of light green, green, and dark green cotton (for leaves and stems)
- 53 ¹/₈" (135 cm) of 1 ³/₈" (3.5 cm) wide bias tape of cream print (for binding)
- 14 ¹/₄" x 14 ¹/₄" (36 x 36 cm) of beige floral print cotton (for backing)
- 14 ¹/₄" x 14 ¹/₄" (36 x 36 cm) of batting
- Scrap of fusible interfacing

Variation 2

- 1 ³/₈" x 22" (3.5 x 56 cm) of navy blue print cotton (for the 1" [2.5 cm] a log cabin pieces)
- ³/₄" x 51 ³/₄" (2 x 130 cm) of navy blue print cotton (for the ³/₈" [1 cm] a log cabin pieces)
- 15 ³/₄" x 15 ³/₄" (40 x 40 cm) of gray print cotton (for pieces b and c)
- 7 ¹/₂" x 7 ¹/₂" (19 x 19 cm) of white and indigo print cotton (for round flower and bud)
- Three 1" x 8 ³/₄" (2.5 x 22 cm) bias strips of blue print cotton (for six-petal flowers)
- 2 ³/₄" x 4" (7 x 10 cm) of light indigo print cotton (for five-petal flowers)
- 4" x 6 ¹/₄" (10 x 16 cm) each of indigo and dark indigo cotton (for leaves and stems)
- 53 ¹/₈" (135 cm) of 1 ³/₈" (3.5 cm) wide bias tape of gray print (for binding)
- 14 ¹/₄" x 14 ¹/₄" (36 x 36 cm) of beige floral print cotton (for backing)
- 14 ¹/₄" x 14 ¹/₄" (36 x 36 cm) of batting
- Scrap of fusible interfacing

Sew using ¹/₄" (0.5 cm) seam allowances, unless otherwise noted.

Construction Steps

1. Make the log cabin block

Make templates for pieces ① and ⑮-⑱ using template on Pattern Sheet B. Cut out the fabric, adding ¼" (0.5 cm) seam allowance. Cut out strips for the remaining log cabin pieces. All strips are either ⅜" (1 cm) or 1" (2.5 cm) wide without seam allowance. This means the pieces should be ¾" (2 cm) or 1⅜" (3.5 cm) wide once seam allowance has been added. Sew the pieces together in numerical order to make a hexagon log cabin block for the basket. With right sides together, sew pieces ⑮-⑱ to the block. Cut out the border pieces following the measurements in the diagram below. Make sure to add ¼" (0.5 cm) seam allowance to all border piece edges. Sew the border pieces to the assembled block.

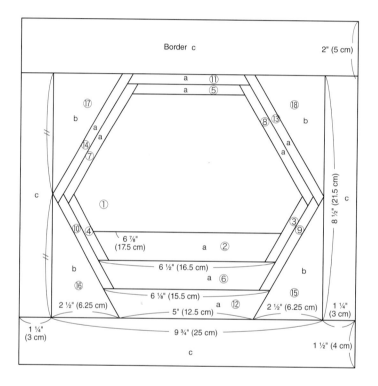

2. Make the stems

Cut ¾" (2 cm) wide bias strips from the stem fabrics. This measurement includes seam allowance. For each stem, fold the bias strip in half with right sides facing out and running stitch ⅛" (0.3 cm) from the fold. Trim the excess fabric, leaving ⅛" (0.3 cm) seam allowance. Fold the bias strip in half again and pin the long edges together. Slip-stitch the edges together. Transfer the appliqué template on the pattern sheet to the log cabin block. Appliqué the stems to the log cabin block.

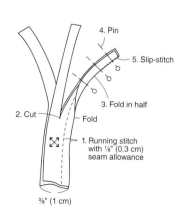

3. Appliqué the leaves

Make templates for the leaves using the template on Pattern Sheet B. Cut out the fabric, adding ¼" (0.4 cm) seam allowance. Appliqué the leaves to the log cabin block following the placement indicated on the pattern sheet.

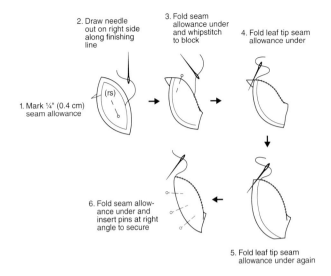

2. Draw needle out on right side along finishing line

3. Fold seam allowance under and whipstitch to block

4. Fold leaf tip seam allowance under

1. Mark ¼" (0.4 cm) seam allowance

(rs)

6. Fold seam allowance under and insert pins at right angle to secure

5. Fold leaf tip seam allowance under again

4. Make the round flower

Cut out a 5 ½" (14 cm) diameter circle. This measurement includes seam allowance. Running stitch around the circle using ¹⁄₁₆" (0.2 cm) seam allowance. Make a 4 ¾" (12 cm) diameter circle template. Insert the template and pull the thread tails to gather the fabric into shape. Remove the template, then running stitch around the circle in a large zigzag pattern. Pull the thread tails to gather the fabric into a flower shape. Press lightly from the right side to adjust the shape, then sew to secure.

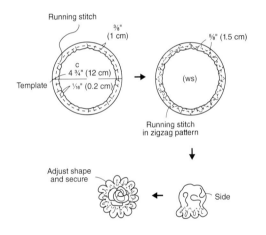

Running stitch

⅜" (1 cm)

⅝" (1.5 cm)

c
4 ¾" (12 cm)

Template

¹⁄₁₆" (0.2 cm)

(ws)

Running stitch in zigzag pattern

Adjust shape and secure

Side

5. Make the bud

Cut out a 1 ¼" (3 cm) diameter circle. This measurement includes seam allowance. Fold the circle in half and running stitch using ¹⁄₁₆" (0.2 cm) seam allowance. Pull to gather the bud into shape, then sew around the base to secure.

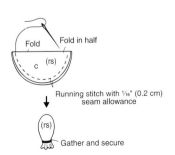

Fold

Fold in half

c   (rs)

Running stitch with ¹⁄₁₆" (0.2 cm) seam allowance

(rs)

Gather and secure

6. Make the six-petal flowers

Use a ½" (1.2 cm) bias tape maker to turn the six-petal flower bias strips into bias tape. Mark the top and bottom seam allowances at 1¼" (3 cm) intervals, as shown in the diagram below. Running stitch in a zigzag pattern to connect the marks. Pull the thread tails to gather the fabric into a flower shape. Make a couple of stitches to join the ends together, then knot to secure. Follow the same process to make two more six-petal flowers.

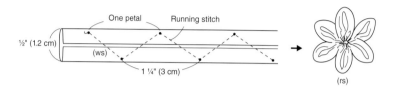

7. Make the five-petal flowers

Cut out a 1¼" (3 cm) diameter circle. This measurement includes seam allowance. Running stitch around the circle using ⅟₁₆" (0.2 cm) seam allowance. Divide the circle into five equal sections and mark the wrong side, as shown in the diagram below. Adhere a ⅛" (0.3 cm) square of interfacing to the wrong side of the center of the circle. Draw the needle out on the right side at the center of the circle. Make a large stitch and reinsert the needle at ①. Draw the needle out on the right side at the center once again. Pull the thread to tighten the stitch and gather the fabric into a petal shape. Follow the same process to make the remaining petals. Make a couple of stitches at the center of the flower to connect the petals, then knot to secure. Follow the same process to make four more five-petal flowers.

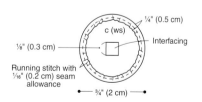
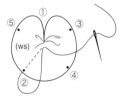
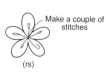

8. Appliqué the flowers and bud

Appliqué the round flower, the bud, the six-petal flowers, and the five-petal flowers to the log cabin block following the placement indicated on the pattern sheet.

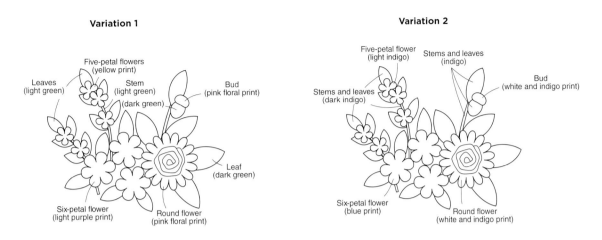

Variation 1

Variation 2

9. Quilt the tapestry

Cut the batting and backing so they are 6" (15 cm) larger than the quilt top. Layer the top, batting, and backing. Baste, then quilt as shown in the diagram below. Follow the instructions on pages 16-20 to bind the tapestry.

Variation 1

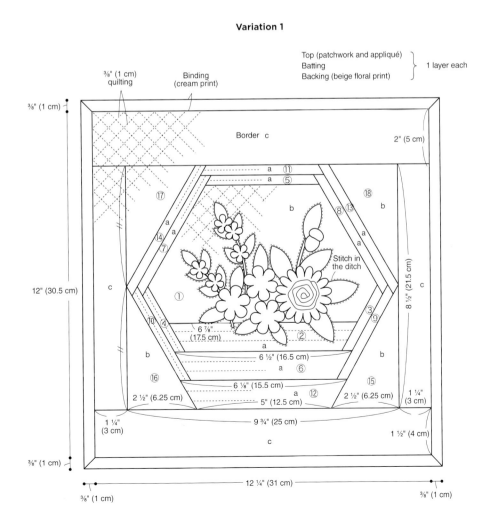

PARALLELOGRAM STAR QUILT

shown on page 78

Finished Size: 60" x 79 ¾" (152.5 x 202.5 cm)

Full-size templates of the parallelogram log cabin blocks are located on Pattern Sheet B.

RECOMMENDED CONSTRUCTION TECHNIQUE:

Parallelogram Log Cabin Block...page 80

Materials

- 43 ½" x 126 ⅛" (110 x 320 cm) of black cotton (for log cabin pieces and pieces a and b)
  - Includes 287 ⅜" (720 cm) of 2" (5 cm) wide bias strips (for binding)
- 43 ¼" x 55" (110 x 140 cm) of light gray cotton (for log cabin pieces)

- 21 ¾" x 23 ⅝" (55 x 60 cm) each of maroon print, green solid, and dark gray solid cotton (for log cabin pieces)
- 21 ¾" x 23 ⅝" (55 x 60 cm) of bluish purple print cotton (for log cabin pieces)

- Scraps of solid and floral print cotton in various colors (for log cabin pieces)
- 65" x 85 ⅝" (165 x 215 cm) of small floral print cotton (for backing)
- 65" x 85 ⅝" (165 x 215 cm) of batting

Sew using ¼" (0.6 cm) seam allowances, unless otherwise noted.

Construction Steps

1. Make the log cabin blocks

Make templates for the log cabin pieces using the templates on Pattern Sheet B. Cut out strips for the log cabin pieces. All strips should be ½" (1.25 cm) wide without seam allowance. This means the pieces will be 1" (2.45 cm) wide once the seam allowance has been added. Sew the pieces together in numerical order to make 54 each of Patterns A and A' and 26 each of Patterns B and B'. Note: A' is the mirror image of A, and B' is the mirror image of B.

Pattern A
(make 54)

Pattern A'
(make 54)

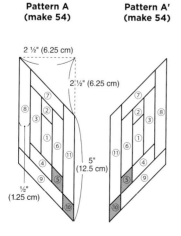

All pieces are ½" (1.25 cm) wide.

Pattern B
(make 26)

Pattern B'
(make 26)

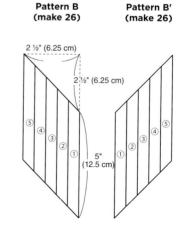

2. Cut out pieces a and b

Cut out 3" (7.5 cm) wide strips for pieces a and b. This measurement includes seam allowance. Refer to the step 3 diagram below for length measurements. Trim the strips into triangles for the b pieces.

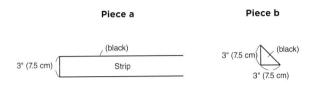

3. Make the rows

Sew Pattern A to A' and B to B' to make the star motifs following the layout in the diagram below. Attach the a and b pieces to complete one row. Follow the same process to complete two additional rows.

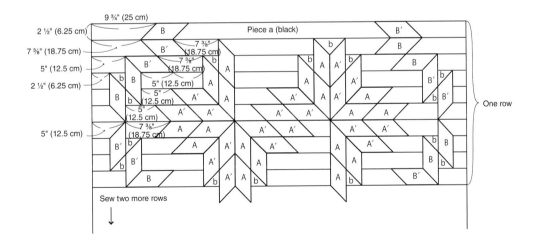

4. Finish the quilt

Cut the batting and backing so they are 6"
(15 cm) larger than the quilt top. Layer the top,
batting, and backing. Baste, then quilt as shown
in the diagrams below. Follow the instructions on
pages 16-20 to bind the tapestry.

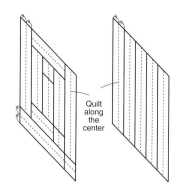

Quilt
along
the
center

Top (patchwork)
Batting } 1 layer each
Backing (small floral print)

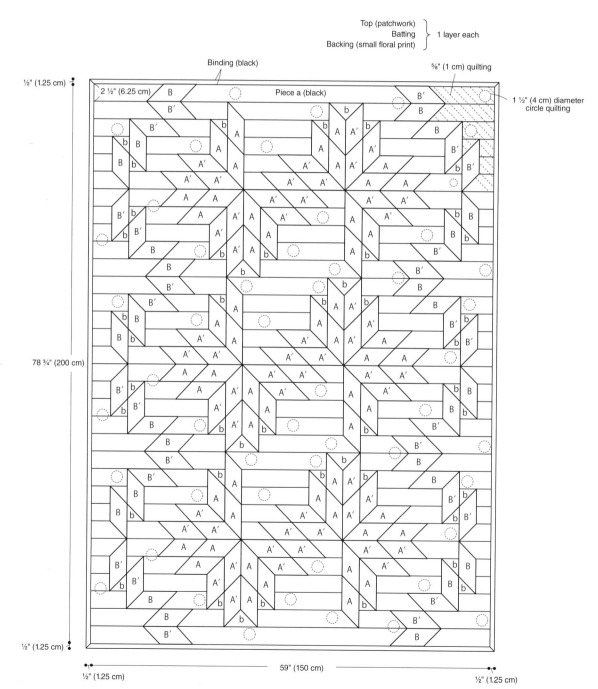

PART THREE

Unique Log Cabin Blocks

Basic log cabin blocks are reinterpreted to create the distinctive designs featured in this collection. Design your own project using the deconstructed log cabin technique explained in the overview on pages 128-141. Or change the width of the strips to create crazy log cabin blocks. This section is all about using the traditional log cabin motif in unexpected ways.

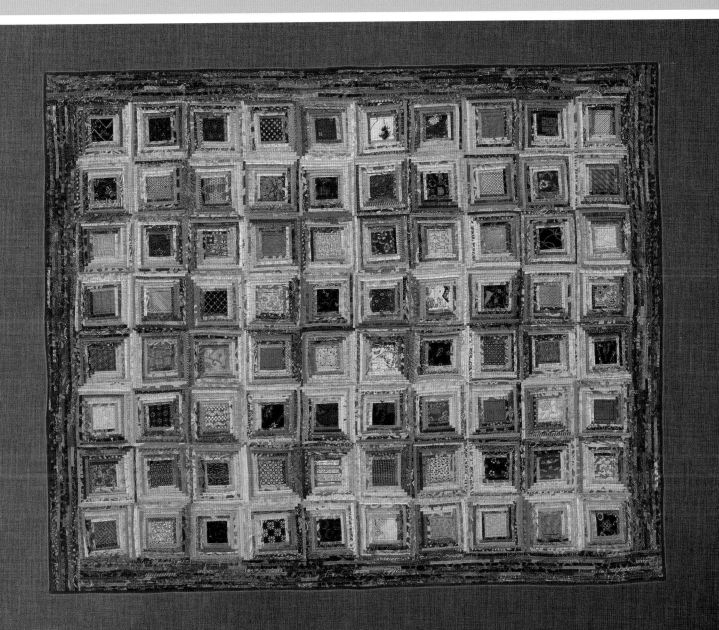

PLAID TOTE

Create this stylish tote with the fun and easy deconstructed log cabin technique. Use an assortment of plaid, checked, and striped fabrics within the same color palette to achieve a balanced overall impression. Leather handles lend the bag a refined feel.

Instructions on page 128

PLAID POUCH

Put your fabric scraps to good use with this little pouch. The deconstructed log cabin technique is perfect for using up scraps of all shapes and sizes.

Instructions on page 137

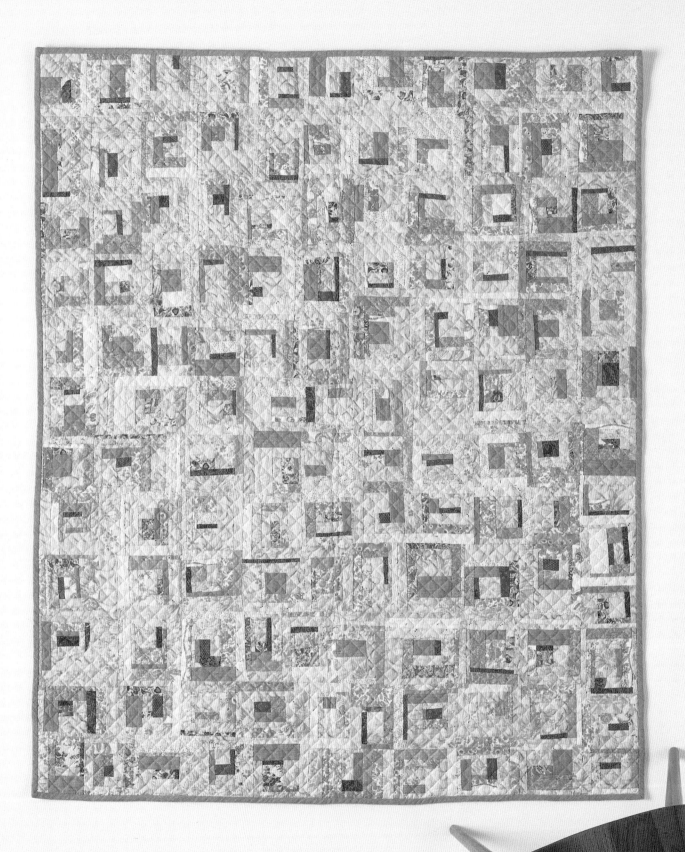

LABYRINTH TAPESTRY

This labyrinth-inspired tapestry is composed of crazy log cabin blocks. Combine light and dark fabrics to achieve balance throughout the quilt. This large tapestry also works well as a sofa cover or rug.

Instructions on page 142

INDIGO & CALICO TAPESTRY

When it comes to log cabin quilts, the more fabrics you include, the better. The blocks in this quilt are composed of narrow strips, then the extra strips are sewn together to make beautiful borders. This quilt contains another special detail: a different fabric is used for the large center piece of each block, creating a catalog of eighty different indigo fabrics.

Instructions on page 144

FLOWER GARDEN QUILT

Inspired by the traditional barn raising motif, this stunning quilt combines floral prints in several different colors to create a garden depicted through fabric. Floral motif quilting templates add a special finishing touch.

Instructions on page 147

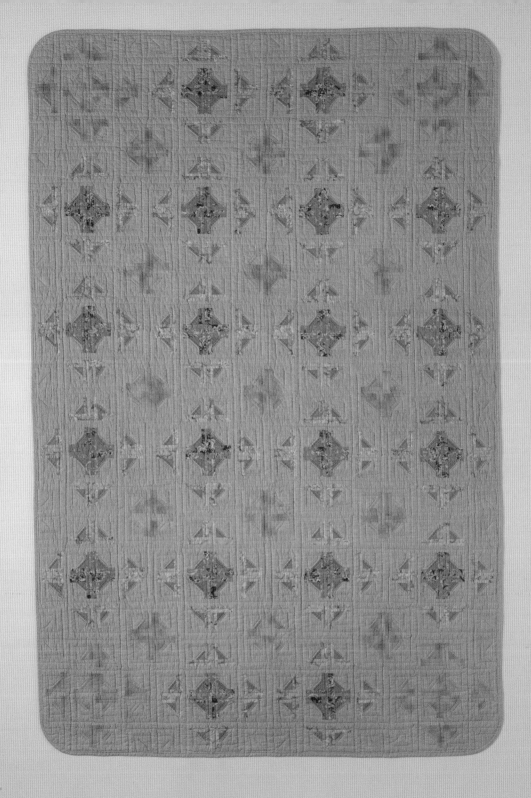

NEUTRAL BEDSPREAD

Neutral, soothing colors, such as the tan and gold used in this bedspread, will promote a good night's rest. A creative fabric layout transforms a basic log cabin motif into this unique design.

Instructions on page 150

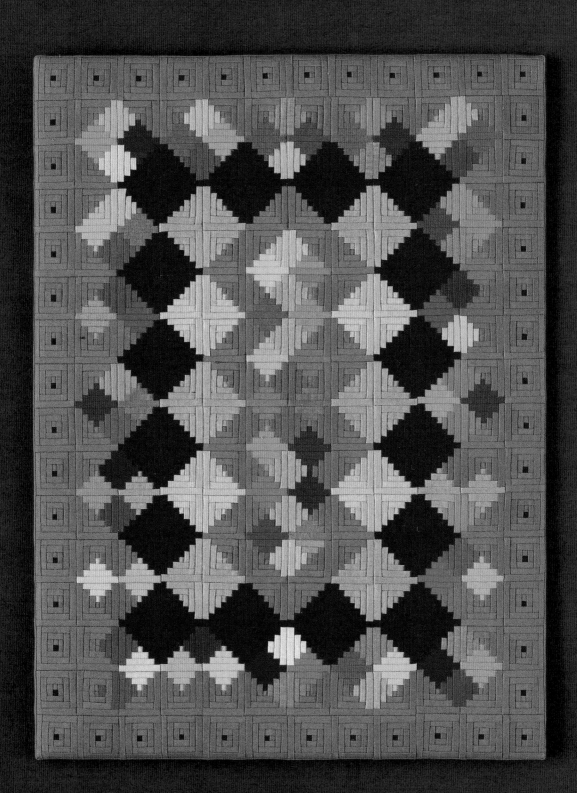

AMISH TAPESTRY

Use solid fabric in Amish-inspired colors of green, red, blue, and purple to create this bold tapestry. This quilt uses the same pattern as the Kimono Bedspread on page 26, yet the solid color scheme and narrower pieces provide this design with a completely different look.

Instructions on page 153

BOUTIS COASTERS

Boutis, a traditional French quilting technique is used to create three-dimensional, stuffed designs at the center of each coaster. Frame the design with a double-sided log cabin block comprised of narrow strips.

Instructions on page 156

LANDSCAPE BLOCKS

Recreate landscapes in fabric form. Use different fabrics and different size pieces to depict your favorite sights.

Instructions on page 160

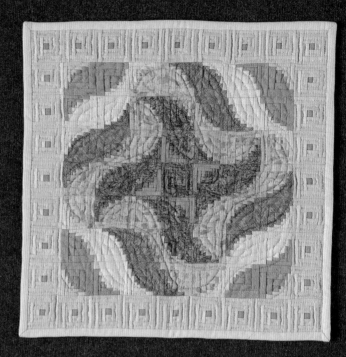

WAVE & LEAF TAPESTRIES

The log cabin blocks used to create each of these tapestries feature a 2:1 width ratio. This unique design feature imparts a feeling of rhythm and movement. The top tapestry is inspired by ocean waves, while the bottom tapestry depicts leaves swaying in the wind.

Instructions on page 162

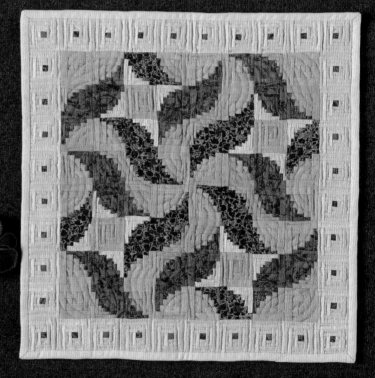

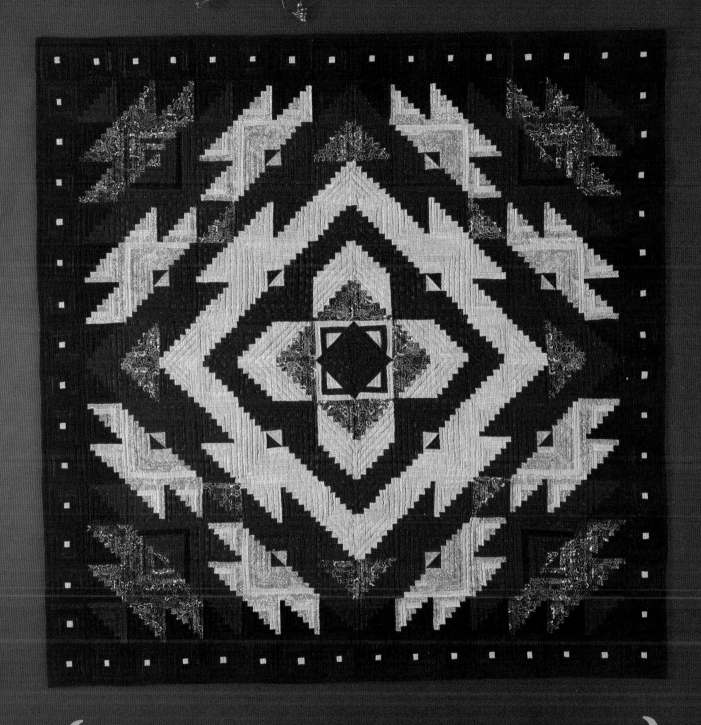

FLYING VULTURE TAPESTRY

A flock of fabric vultures appeared as I began sewing the pieces of this quilt together, lending this design its distinctive name. This design is most striking when worked in contrasting colors, such as the maroon, red, and beige pictured here.

Instructions on page 165

HOW TO MAKE DECONSTRUCTED LOG CABIN BLOCKS

PLAID TOTE

shown on page 114

Finished Size: 10 ³/₄" x 13 ³/₄" (27.5 x 35 cm)

A full-size template is located on Pattern Sheet B.

Materials

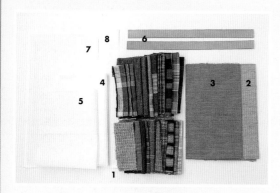

1. 18-19 different plaid, checked, and striped indigo and neutral cottons (for log cabin pieces)
2. 13 ³/₄" x 35 ¹/₂" (35 x 90 cm) of gray cotton (for log cabin pieces, borders, facings, and pocket flap)
3. 14 ¹/₂" x 25 ¹/₂" (37 x 65 cm) of brown cotton (for lining and pocket)
4. 21 ³/₄" x 30" (55 x 76 cm) of lightweight fusible interfacing
5. 14 ¹/₂" x 24 ¹/₂" (37 x 62 cm) of heavyweight fusible interfacing
6. Two 13 ³/₄" (35 cm) long pieces of 1" (2.5 cm) wide leather (about ¹/₁₆" [0.2 cm] thick)
7. Three or four sheets of tracing paper
8. Three sheets of graph paper

Project Diagrams

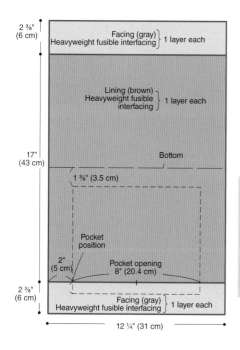

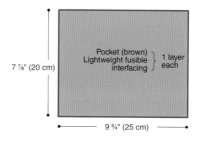

Add ³/₈" (1 cm) seam allowance to the lining, facings, and heavyweight fusible interfacing for these pieces.

Do not add seam allowance to the pocket, pocket flap, or lightweight fusible interfacing for these pieces.

Add ³⁄₈" (0.75 cm) seam allowance to all top patchwork pieces and the lightweight fusible interfacing. Add ³⁄₈" (1 cm) seam allowance to all border pieces.

Top (patchwork + border) ⎫ 1 layer each
Lightweight fusible interfacing ⎭

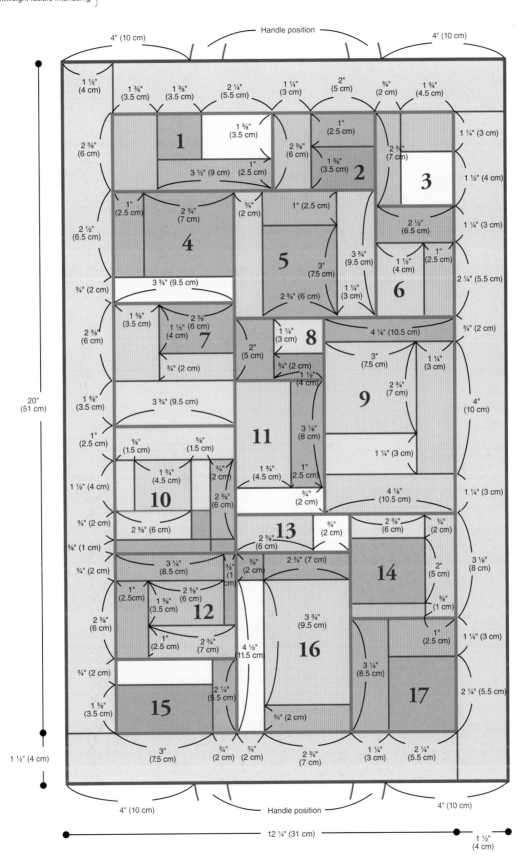

Handle position

4" (10 cm)   4" (10 cm)

1 ½"
(4 cm)
1 ³⁄₈"   1 ³⁄₈"   2 ¼"   1 ¼"   2"   ³⁄₄"   1 ¾"
(3.5 cm) (3.5 cm) (5.5 cm) (3 cm) (5 cm) (2 cm) (4.5 cm)

2 ³⁄₈"
(6 cm)

1   1 ³⁄₈"
(3.5 cm)   1"
(2.5 cm)   1 ¼" (3 cm)

2 ³⁄₈"
(6 cm)   1 ³⁄₈"
(3.5 cm)   **2**   2 ¾"
(7 cm)   **3**   1 ½" (4 cm)

3 ½" (9 cm)   1"
(2.5 cm)

2 ½"
(6.5 cm)

1"
(2.5 cm)   2 ¾"
(7 cm)   ³⁄₄"
(2 cm)   1" (2.5 cm)   2 ½"
(6.5 cm)   1 ¼" (3 cm)

4   **5**   3"
(7.5 cm)   3 ¾"
(9.5 cm)   1"
(2.5 cm)

1 ½"
(4 cm)

³⁄₄" (2 cm)   3 ¾" (9.5 cm)   2 ³⁄₈" (6 cm)   1 ¼"
(3 cm)   **6**   2 ¼" (5.5 cm)

2 ³⁄₈"
(6 cm)   1 ³⁄₈"
(3.5 cm)   2 ³⁄₈" (6 cm)   1 ¼"
(3 cm)   ³⁄₄" (2 cm)

1 ½"
(4 cm)   **7**   2"
(5 cm)   **8**   4 ⅛" (10.5 cm)

³⁄₄" (2 cm)   ³⁄₄" (2 cm)   1 ½"
(4 cm)   3"
(7.5 cm)   1 ¼"
(3 cm)

20"
(51 cm)

1 ³⁄₈"
(3.5 cm)   3 ¾" (9.5 cm)   **9**   2 ¾"
(7 cm)   4"
(10 cm)

1"
(2.5 cm)   ⅝"
(1.5 cm)   ⅝"
(1.5 cm)   **11**   3 ⅛"
(8 cm)

1 ½" (4 cm)   1 ¾"
(4.5 cm)   ³⁄₄"
(2 cm)   1 ¾"
(4.5 cm)   1"
(2.5 cm)   1 ¼" (3 cm)

10   2 ³⁄₈"
(6 cm)   ³⁄₄"
(2 cm)   4 ⅛"
(10.5 cm)   1 ¼" (3 cm)

³⁄₄" (2 cm)   2 ³⁄₈" (6 cm)   **13**   ³⁄₄"
(2 cm)   2 ³⁄₈"
(6 cm)   ³⁄₄"
(2 cm)

³⁄₈" (1 cm)   3 ¼"
(8.5 cm)   ³⁄₈"
(1 cm)   ³⁄₄"
(2 cm)   2 ¾" (7 cm)   3 ⅛"
(8 cm)

³⁄₄" (2 cm)   2 ³⁄₈"
(6 cm)   **14**   2"
(5 cm)

1"
(2.5cm)   2 ³⁄₈"
(6 cm)   1 ³⁄₈"
(3.5 cm)   **12**   ⅜"
(1 cm)

2 ³⁄₈"
(6 cm)   3 ¾"
(9.5 cm)   1"
(2.5 cm)   1 ¼" (3 cm)

1"
(2.5 cm)   2 ¾"
(7 cm)   4 ½"
11.5 cm)   **16**

³⁄₄" (2 cm)   2 ¼"
(5.5 cm)   3 ¼"
(8.5 cm)   **17**   2 ¼" (5.5 cm)

1 ³⁄₈"
(3.5 cm)   **15**   ³⁄₄" (2 cm)

1 ½" (4 cm)   3"
(7.5 cm)   ³⁄₄"
(2 cm)   ³⁄₄"
(2 cm)   2 ¾"
(7 cm)   1 ¼"
(3 cm)   2 ¼"
(5.5 cm)

Handle position

4" (10 cm)   4" (10 cm)

12 ¼" (31 cm)   1 ½"
(4 cm)

Construction Steps

1. Make the blocks

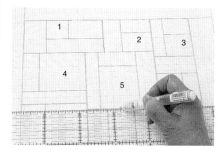

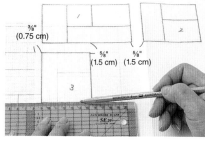

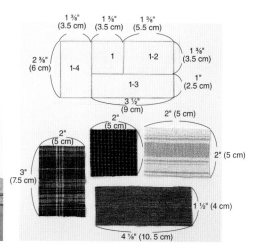

1. Transfer the template on Pattern Sheet B onto graph paper or draw your own diagram. Use a highlighter to outline each block, then label the block numbers.

2. Transfer onto tracing paper, leaving about ⅝" (1.5 cm) space between each block. Add ⅜" (0.75 cm) seam allowance around each block, then cut out the foundation paper template.

3. Cut each piece out of fabric, adding ⅜" (0.75 cm) seam allowance around each edge. Pay attention when cutting striped or checked fabric so the pattern is oriented in the same direction for all pieces.

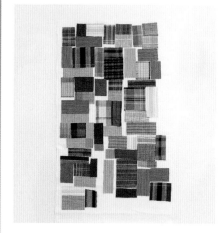

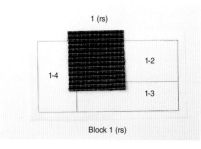

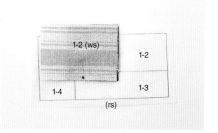

4. Lay out the fabric pieces following the diagram on page 129. Make sure the different colors and patterns are evenly distributed throughout the work.

5. Position piece ① on section 1 of the foundation paper template. Pin the fabric in place, maintaining an even ⅜" (0.75 cm) seam allowance on all sides.

6. With right sides together, position piece ② on top of piece ① so the fabrics are aligned along the right edge.

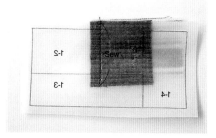

Note: A contrasting color of thread was used in these photos for the purpose of visual clarity. When making this project, select thread in a shade that coordinates with the fabric.

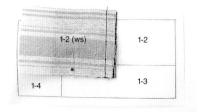

7. Flip the work over so the foundation paper template is facing up. Stitch along the line to sew pieces ① and ② to the paper. Use a short stitch length and do not backstitch.

8. Completed view of step 7 from the right side.

9. Open pieces ① and ②. Finger press the seam allowance to one side.

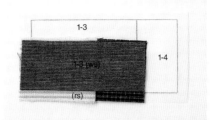

10. With right sides together, position piece ③ on top of the set from step 9 so the fabrics are aligned along the top edge.

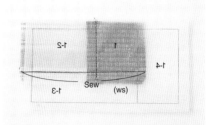

11. Flip the work over and stitch along the line to sew piece ③ to the set from step 9.

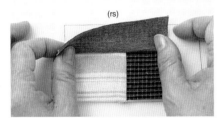

12. Open the pieces. Finger press the seam allowance, being careful not to stretch the fabric.

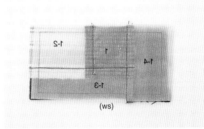

13. Follow the same process to attach piece ④.

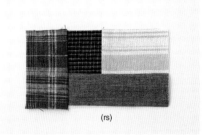

14. Completed view of the block from the right side.

15. Follow the same process to make the remaining blocks.

2. Make the bag top

Note: Seam allowance is ³⁄₈"
(0.75 cm), unless otherwise
noted.

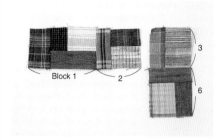

1. Sew blocks 1 and 2 with right
sides together. Sew blocks 3 and 6
with right sides together.

2. Follow the same process to
attach equally sized blocks, as
shown at left.

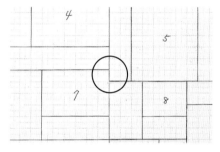

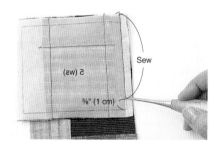

3. Blocks 4 and 5 will need to be attached using a different process since they are different sizes. With right
sides together, position block 5 on top of block 4 so the fabrics are aligned along the top and right edges. Sew
the blocks together, leaving the bottom ³⁄₈" (1 cm) unattached.

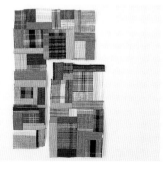

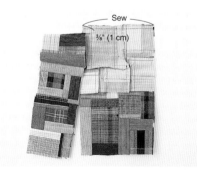

4. Sew blocks 1-7, 10, 12, and 15
together. Then sew blocks 8, 9, 11,
14, 16, and 17 together to create
another large section.

5. Align the two sections with
right sides together and sew along
the shorter edge.

6. With right sides together, sew
the two sections together along
the vertical edge.

7. Completed view of the right side once all of the blocks have been sewn together.

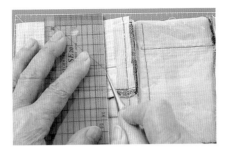

8. Align a ruler next to each line of stitching. Use a stiletto to score a line in the foundation paper template.

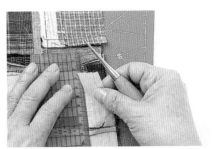

9. Hold the ruler in place with one hand and carefully remove the paper with the other. Remove all of the paper and trim the excess seam allowance. Press the bag top from the right side.

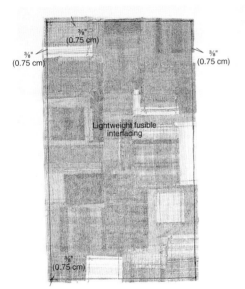

10. Adhere lightweight fusible interfacing to the wrong side of the bag top. Mark the seam allowance ³⁄₈" (0.75 cm) from each edge.

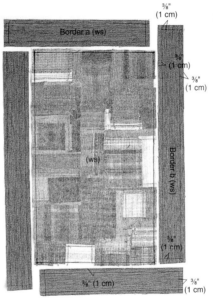

11. Cut out borders a and b following the dimensions in the diagram on page 129. Make sure to add ³⁄₈" (1 cm) seam allowance around each border piece edge. Adhere lightweight interfacing to the wrong side of each piece.

12. With right sides together, sew the borders to the bag top, following the order indicated in the photo. Refer to the diagram on page 134 for detailed instructions on attaching the borders.

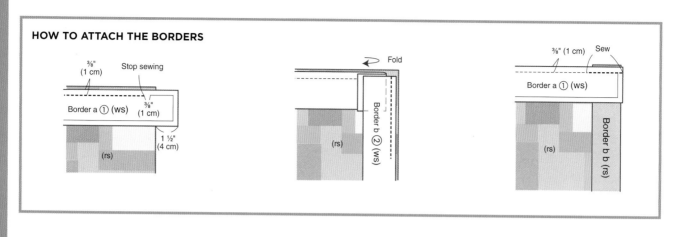

HOW TO ATTACH THE BORDERS

3. Sew the bag together

1. Cut out the lining and facings, adding ³/₈" (1 cm) seam allowance to each edge. Cut out pieces of heavyweight fusible interfacing to match. Adhere each piece of interfacing to the wrong side of the fabric.

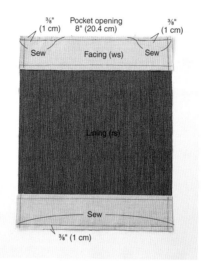

2. Align the facings and lining with right sides together. Sew the upper facing to the lining from edge to edge, leaving an 8" (20.4 cm) opening. Sew the lower facing to the lining from edge to edge.

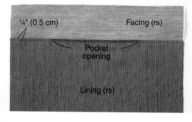

3. Turn the facings right side out. Topstitch the lining underneath the upper facing.

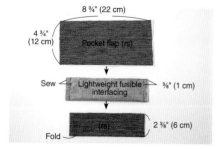

4. Cut out the pocket flap and lightweight fusible interfacing. Adhere the interfacing to the wrong side of the fabric. Fold the pocket flap in half with right sides together. Sew along both short edges, stitching from edge to edge. Turn right side out and press.

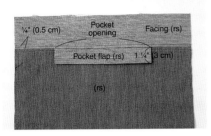

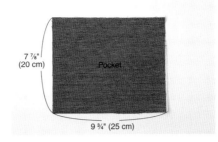

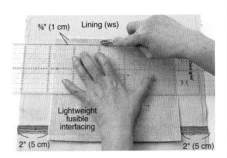

5. Insert half of the pocket flap into the pocket opening. Topstitch the facing to secure the pocket flap.

6. Cut out the pocket and light-weight fusible interfacing. Adhere the interfacing to the wrong side of the fabric.

7. Align the right side of the pocket with the wrong side of the lining, following the placement indicated in the diagram on page 128. Mark the seam allowance lines along all four sides of the pocket.

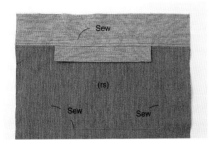

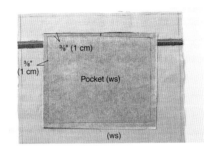

8. Working from the right side of the lining, sew along the seam allowance lines to attach the pocket.

4. Attach the handles

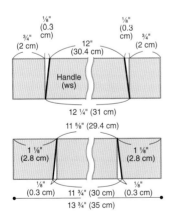

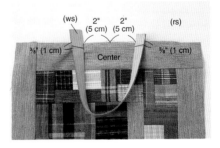

1. Mark the short ends of the leather handles, following the measurements in the diagram above. Note: One handle will be shorter than the other to make the bag easier to carry.

2. Adhere pieces of double-sided tape on the right side of each handle in the same positions as the marks on the wrong side.

3. Remover paper backing from the double-sided tape. With right sides together, adhere the handles to the bag top using the marks as a guide.

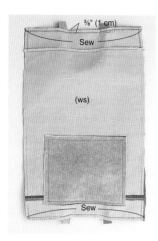

4. Align the bag top and lining with right sides together and the handles sandwiched in between the two layers of fabric. Sew across the short sides of the bag, stitching from edge to edge.

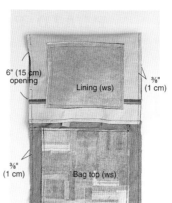

5. Separate the two layers of fabric and fold both the bag top and lining in half. Sew along the long sides of the bag, stitching from edge to edge and leaving a 6" (15 cm) opening on one side.

6. Turn the bag right side out through the opening.

7. Whipstitch the opening in the lining.

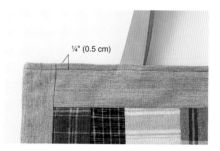

8. Insert the lining inside the bag and press into shape. Topstitch around the opening edge of the bag.

Variations

RECYCLED

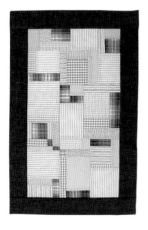

Cut large pieces out from old men's shirts. Use a dark border to frame the patchwork.

COUNTRY

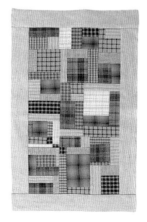

Use shades of brown to create a country-style bag. Accents of light beige check fabric lighten the overall tone.

MODERN

Combine solids and patterns for a high contrast look. Mixing new and vintage fabric further accentuates the contrast.

PLAID POUCH

shown on page 115

Finished Size: 6 ½" x 8 ¾" (16.5 x 22 cm)

A full-size template is located on Pattern Sheet B.

Materials

1. 18-19 different plaid, checked, and striped indigo and neutral cottons (for log cabin pieces)
2. One 1 ¼" x 23 ⅝" (3 x 60 cm) solid indigo cotton bias strip (for binding and loop)
3. 9 ½" x 13 ¾" (24 x 35 cm) of lightweight fusible interfacing
4. 13 ¾" x 16 ⅛" (35 x 42 cm) of navy print cotton (for lining and pocket)
5. One ¾" (2 cm) square button
6. One 4" (10 cm) long piece of ¼" (0.5 cm) wide flat elastic tape

Project Diagrams

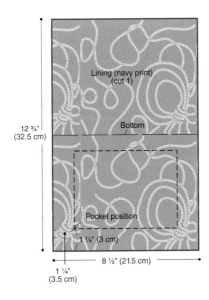

Lining (navy print) (cut 1)

Bottom

Pocket position

12 ¾" (32.5 cm)

8 ½" (21.5 cm)

1 ¼" (3 cm)

1 ¼" (3.5 cm)

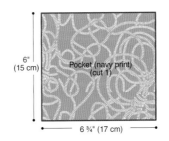

Pocket (navy print) (cut 1)

6" (15 cm)

6 ¾" (17 cm)

Do not add seam allowance to the pocket.

Add ⅜" (0.75 cm) seam allowance to the lining.

Top (patchwork)
Lightweight fusible interfacing } 1 layer each

Add ³⁄₈″ (0.75 cm) seam allowance to all top patchwork pieces and the lightweight fusible interfacing.

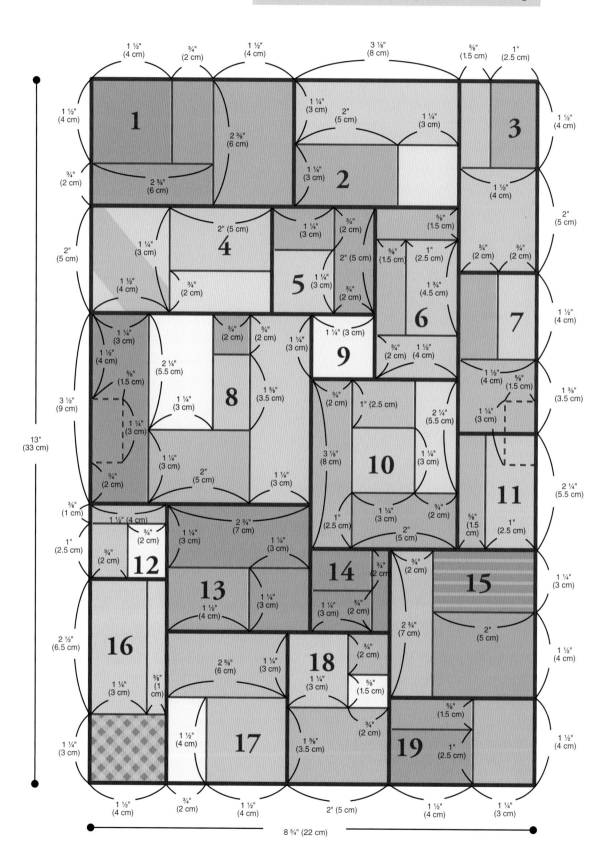

1. Make the pouch top

Refer to pages 36-37 for instructions on sewing the patchwork pieces together using the paper piecing technique.

(rs)

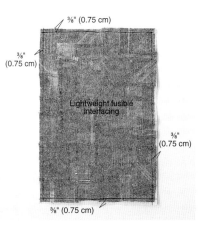

⅜" (0.75 cm)

⅜" (0.75 cm)

Lightweight fusible interfacing

⅜" (0.75 cm)

⅜" (0.75 cm)

1. Sew the blocks together to make the pouch top, following the same process used on pages 130-133.

2. Remove the foundation paper template. Adhere lightweight fusible interfacing to the wrong side of the pouch top. Mark the seam allowance ⅜" (0.75 cm) from each edge.

2. Sew the pouch together

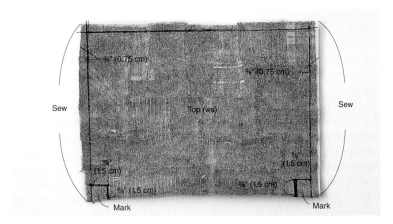

⅜" (0.75 cm)

⅜" (0.75 cm)

Sew

Top (ws)

Sew

⅝" (1.5 cm)

⅝" (1.5 cm)

⅝" (1.5 cm)

⅝" (1.5 cm)

Mark

Mark

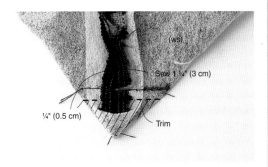

(ws)

Sew 1 ¼" (3 cm)

¼" (0.5 cm)

Trim

1. Fold the pouch top in half with right sides together. Sew across the two sides, stitching from edge to edge. Press the seam allowances open. Mark each corner ⅝" (1.5 cm) from the side seam allowance and bottom.

2. Align each side seam with the bottom, forming the corners into triangles. Sew across each corner with a 1 ¼" (3 cm) long seam, following the mark as a guide. Trim the excess, leaving ¼" (0.5 cm) seam allowance.

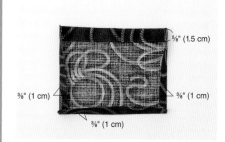

Lining (rs)

Lining (ws)

Corner   Corner

3. Fold the opening edge of the pocket over ⅝" (1.5 cm) twice and topstitch. Fold the other three edges over ⅜" (1 cm) and press.

4. Topstitch the pocket to the right side of the lining, following the placement indicated in the diagram on page 137.

5. Fold the lining in half with right sides together. Sew along the two sides, stitching from edge to edge using ⅜" (0.75 cm) seam allowance. Miter each corner following the same process used in step 2 on page 139.

Top (ws)

Hand sew

Lining (ws)

6. Hand sew the corner seam allowance to secure. Position the pouch top and lining corner seam allowance in opposite directions so they don't overlap.

3. Make the loop

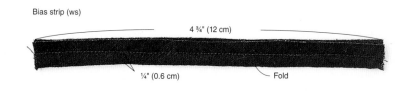

Bias strip (ws)

4 ¾" (12 cm)

¼" (0.6 cm)   Fold

1. Cut a 4 ¾" (12 cm) long piece from the bias strip. Fold in half with right sides together and sew ¼" (0.6 cm) from the fold.

2. Turn right side out using a loop turner.

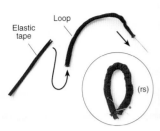

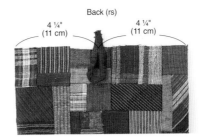

3. Use a needle and thread to insert the elastic tape through the bias strip tube. Form the tube into a loop and pin the ends together.

4. Sew the loop to the back of the pouch, following the placement indicated in the photo above.

4. Bind the opening

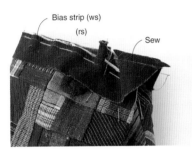

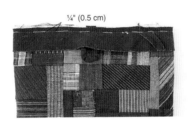

1. Insert the lining into the pouch top. With right sides together, baste the bias strip to the pouch opening, leaving 2"-2 ⅜" (5-6 cm) unattached on both ends. Machine stitch the unattached ends of the bias strip together.

2. Machine stitch the bias strip to the pouch. Trim the pouch seam allowances to match the bias strip seam allowances.

3. Wrap the bias strip around the seam allowance. Slip-stitch the bias strip to the lining.

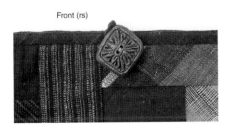

4. Sew the button to the front.

5. Completed view of the pouch.

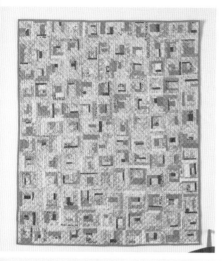

LABYRINTH TAPESTRY

shown on page 116

Finished Size: 44" x 52" (112 x 132 cm)

RECOMMENDED CONSTRUCTION TECHNIQUE:

Deconstructed Log Cabin...page 130

Materials

- Scraps of assorted cotton prints (for log cabin pieces)
- 196 ⁷⁄₈" (200 cm) of 1 ³⁄₈" (3.5 cm) wide bias strips of beige striped cotton (for binding)
- 49 ¹⁄₄" x 57" (125 x 145 cm) of floral print cotton (for backing)
- 49 ¹⁄₄" x 57" (125 x 145 cm) of batting

Sew using ¹⁄₄" (0.6 cm) seam allowances, unless otherwise noted.

Construction Steps

1. Make the log cabin blocks

Draw crazy log cabin blocks, following the dimensions provided in the diagram on the opposite page. Cut out log cabin pieces of various widths from the assorted prints, adding ¹⁄₄" (0.6 cm) seam allowance around each edge. Sew the pieces into blocks using the deconstructed log cabin paper piecing method on pages 130-131.

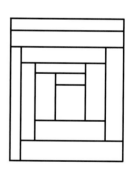

2. Finish the quilt

Follow the same process used on pages 132-133 to sew the blocks together into the quilt top. When attaching blocks of different sizes, use the inset seam method shown in steps 3-6 on page 132. Cut the batting and backing so they are 6" (15 cm) larger than the quilt top. Layer the top, batting, and backing. Baste, then quilt as desired. Follow the instructions on pages 16-20 to bind the tapestry.

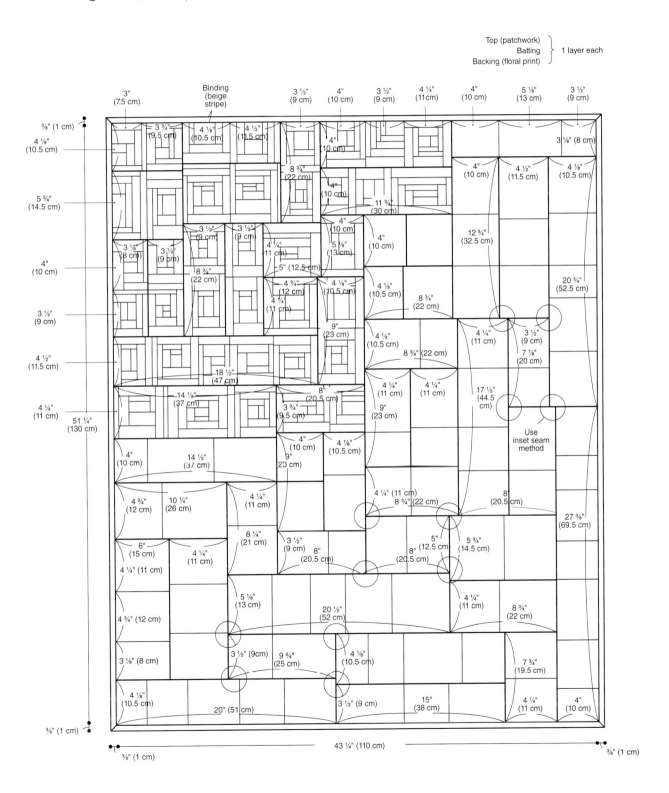

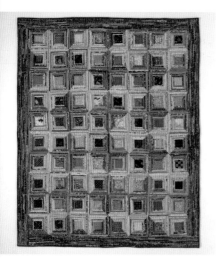

INDIGO & CALICO TAPESTRY

shown on page 118

Finished Size: 71 ⁷⁄₈" x 87 ⁵⁄₈" (182.5 x 222.5 cm)

RECOMMENDED CONSTRUCTION TECHNIQUE:

Method A:
Hand Piece...page 32

Materials

- Scraps of several dozen assorted indigo cottons (for log cabin pieces and borders)
- Scraps of several dozen assorted calicos (for log cabin pieces)
- 324 ⁷⁄₈" (825 cm) of 2" (5 cm) wide bias strips of indigo (for binding)

- 76 ³⁄₄" x 92 ¹⁄₂" (195 x 235 cm) of print cotton (for backing)
- 76 ³⁄₄" x 92 ¹⁄₂" (195 x 235 cm) of batting

Sew using ³⁄₈" (1 cm) seam allowances, unless otherwise noted.

Construction Steps

1. Make the log cabin blocks

Make templates for the center sections of the blocks. Cut out the pieces, adding ³⁄₈" (1 cm) seam allowance. Cut out strips for the remaining log cabin block pieces. All strips should be ³⁄₈" (1 cm) wide without seam allowance. This means that the pieces will be 1 ¹⁄₄" (3 cm) wide once the seam allowance has been added. Sew the pieces together in numerical order to make 40 of each Pattern A and B.

Pattern A (make 40)   **Pattern B (make 40)**

All pieces are ³⁄₈" (1 cm) wide, except for center piece ①.

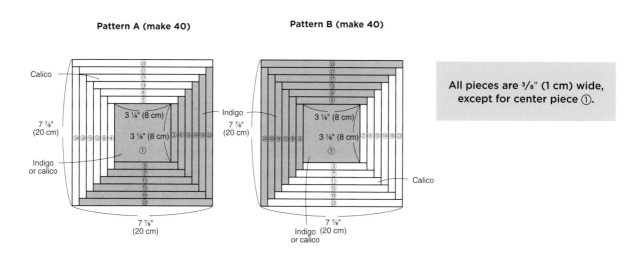

2. Sew the blocks together

Sew two Pattern A and two Pattern B blocks together to create a large block, following the layout indicated in the diagram below. Follow the same process to make a total of 20 large blocks.

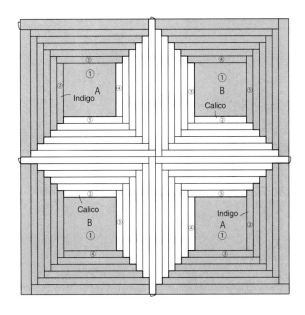

3. Make the borders

Sew leftover ³/₄" (2 cm) wide indigo strips together in groups of 10 using ³/₈" (1 cm) seam allowance. Make two 4 ¹/₄" x 67 ³/₄" (11 x 172 cm) a borders and two 4 ¹/₄" x 83 ¹/₂" (11 x 212 cm) b borders.

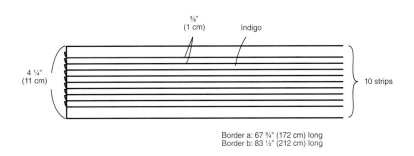

Border a: 67 ¾" (172 cm) long
Border b: 83 ½" (212 cm) long

4. Finish the quilt

Sew the large blocks together in rows of four, following the layout indicated in the diagram below. Sew the rows together, then attach the borders. Cut the batting and backing so they are 6" (15 cm) larger than the quilt top. Layer the top, batting, and backing. Baste, then quilt along the center of each log cabin piece and around the outline of each center piece. Follow the instructions on pages 16-20 to bind the tapestry.

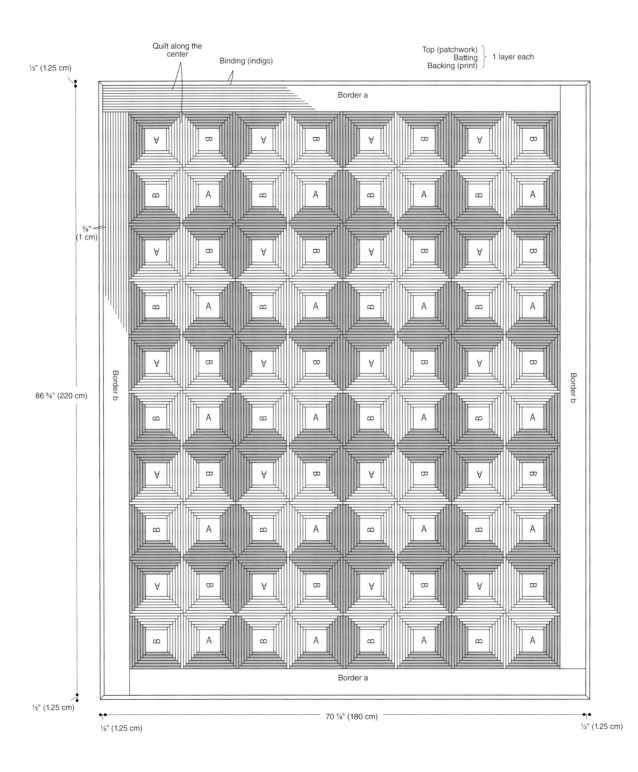

FLOWER GARDEN QUILT

shown on page 120

Finished Size: 58 ⁷⁄₈" x 64 ⁵⁄₈" (149.5 x 164.2 cm)

Full-size quilting templates are located on Pattern Sheet B.

RECOMMENDED CONSTRUCTION TECHNIQUE:

Method B: Machine Stitch...page 34

Materials

- a: 43 ¼" x 47 ¼" (110 x 120 cm) of four different brown floral print cottons (for log cabin pieces)
  - Includes 256" (650 cm) of 2" (5 cm) wide bias strips (for binding)
- b: 43 ¼" x 43 ¼" (110 x 110 cm) of beige floral print cotton (for log cabin pieces)
- c: 35 ½" x 43 ¼" (90 x 110 cm) of white floral print cotton (for log cabin pieces)

- d: 29 ½" x 43 ¼" (75 x 110 cm) of yellow floral print cotton (for log cabin pieces)
- e: 30 ¼" x 43 ¼" (77 x 110 cm) of blue floral print cotton (for log cabin pieces)
- f: 25 ½" x 43 ¼" (65 x 110 cm) of small white floral print cotton (for log cabin pieces)
- g: 19 ¾" x 43 ¼" (50 x 110 cm) of pink floral print cotton (for log cabin pieces)

- h: 21 ¾" x 39 ⅜" (55 x 100 cm) of white solid cotton (for log cabin pieces)
- i: 11 ¾" x 21 ¾" (30 x 55 cm) of green floral print cotton (for log cabin pieces)
- 63 ¾" x 69 ½" (162 x 176.7 cm) of small floral print (for backing)
- 63 ¾" x 69 ½" (162 x 176.7 cm) of batting

Sew using ¼" (0.6 cm) seam allowances, unless otherwise noted.

Construction Steps

1. Make the log cabin blocks

Cut out strips for the log cabin pieces. All strips should be ⁵⁄₈" (1.5 cm) wide without seam allowance. This means that the pieces will be 1 ⅛" (2.7 cm) wide once the seam allowance has been added. Sew the pieces together in numerical order to make 164 of Pattern A and 10 of Pattern B.

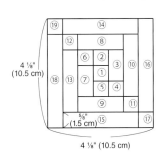

Pattern A (make 164)

4 ⅛" (10.5 cm)

⁵⁄₈" (1.5 cm)

4 ⅛" (10.5 cm)

Refer to diagram on page 148 for Pattern A fabric layout.

Pattern B (make 10)

4 ⅛" (10.5 cm)

⁵⁄₈" (1.5 cm)

4 ⅛" (10.5 cm)

All pieces are ⁵⁄₈" (1.5 cm) wide.

Piece	Fabric
① ④ ⑥ ⑪ ⑫ ⑰ ⑲	pink floral print
All others	white

2. Start sewing the blocks together

Sew three rows of Pattern A blocks together to make each half of the quilt's upper left corner. Sew the two halves together.

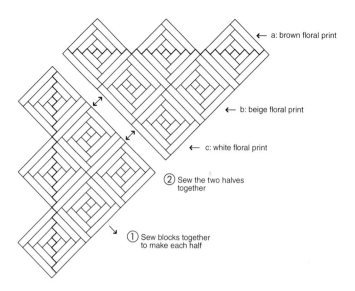

← a: brown floral print

← b: beige floral print

← c: white floral print

② Sew the two halves together

① Sew blocks together to make each half

3. Finish the quilt top

Continue attaching rows of log cabin blocks to complete the quilt top. Trim the quilt top according to the finished dimensions in the diagram on the opposite page, adding ³/₈"- ⁵/₈" (1-1.5 cm) seam allowance.

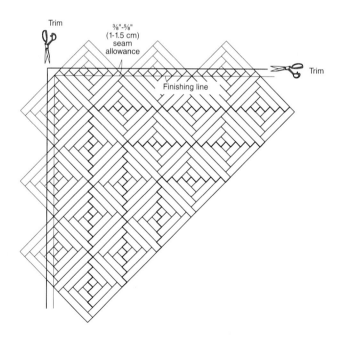

Trim

³/₈"-⁵/₈" (1-1.5 cm) seam allowance

Finishing line

Trim

4. Finish the quilt

Cut the batting and backing so they are 6" (15 cm) larger than the quilt top. Layer the top, batting, and backing. Baste, then use the templates on Pattern Sheet B to quilt as shown in the diagram below. Follow the instructions on pages 16-20 to bind the quilt.

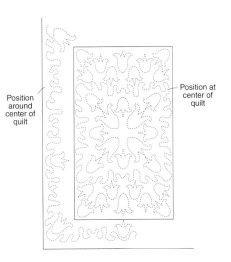

Position around center of quilt

Position at center of quilt

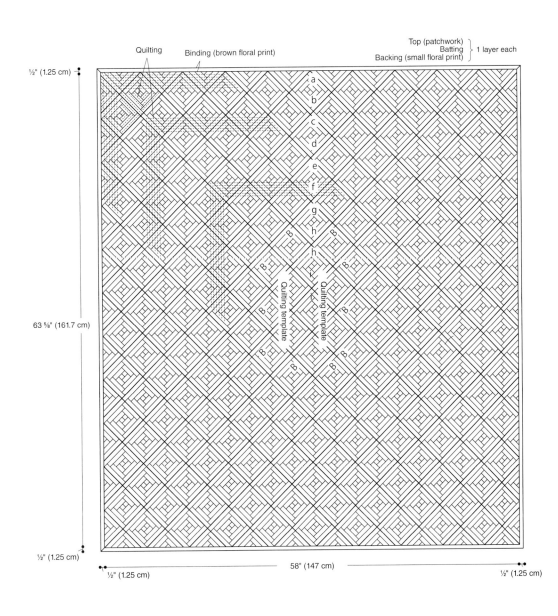

Quilting

Binding (brown floral print)

Top (patchwork)
Batting
Backing (small floral print)
} 1 layer each

½" (1.25 cm)

a
b
c
d
e
f
g
h
h
i

Quilting template

Quilting template

63 ⅝" (161.7 cm)

½" (1.25 cm)

58" (147 cm)

½" (1.25 cm)

½" (1.25 cm)

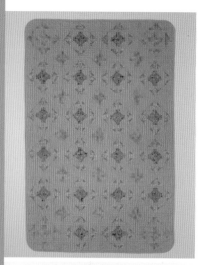

NEUTRAL BEDSPREAD

shown on page 121

Finished Size: 70 ¼" x 105" (178.5 x 266.5 cm)

**RECOMMENDED
CONSTRUCTION
TECHNIQUE:**

Method B: Machine
Stitch...page 34

Materials

- a: 23 ⅝" x 43 ¼" (60 x 110 cm) of orange floral print cotton (for log cabin pieces)
- b: 6" x 43 ¼" (15 x 110 cm) of orange check cotton (for log cabin pieces)
- c: 43 ¼" x 57" (110 x 145 cm) of beige floral print cotton (for log cabin pieces)
- d: 6" x 43 ¼" (15 x 110 cm) of light purple check cotton (for log cabin pieces)

- e: 39 ½" x 43 ¼" (100 x 110 cm) of beige check cotton (for log cabin pieces)
- 43 ¼" x 220 ½" (110 x 560 cm) of beige solid cotton (for log cabin pieces and binding)
- 75 ¼" x 109 ⅞" (191 x 271 cm) of print cotton (for backing)
- 75 ¼" x 109 ⅞" (191 x 271 cm) of batting

Sew using ¼" (0.5 cm) seam allowances, unless otherwise noted.

Construction Steps

1. Make the log cabin blocks

Make templates for pieces ① and ②.
Cut out the pieces, adding ¼" (0.5 cm)
seam allowance. Cut out strips for the
remaining log cabin pieces. All strips
should be 1" (2.5 cm) wide without
seam allowance. This means that the
pieces will be 1 ⅜" (3.5 cm) wide once
the seam allowance has been added.
Sew the pieces together in numerical
order to make 384 of Pattern A. Refer
to the diagrams on the opposite page
for fabric layouts.

Pattern A (make 384)

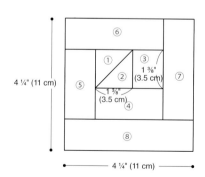

All pieces are 1" (2.5 cm) wide, unless otherwise noted.

2. Make the A Blocks

Sew 16 of Pattern A together to complete Block A, following the layout indicated in the diagrams below. Note: The Block Orientation Diagram applies to Blocks A, B, and C. Make a total of eight A Blocks.

Block A (make 8)

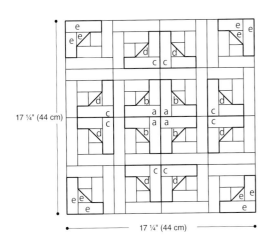

Block Orientation Diagram

Fabric Layout Key
a: orange floral print
b: orange check
c: beige floral print
d: light purple check
e: beige check
unlabeled: beige solid

3. Make the B Blocks

Follow the same process to make a total of 12 B blocks. Refer to the Fabric Layout Key and Block Orientation Diagram above for the B blocks.

4. Make the C Blocks

Follow the same process to make a total of four C blocks. Refer to the Block Orientation Diagram above for layout. Note: These blocks are composed of just two fabrics.

Block B (make 12)

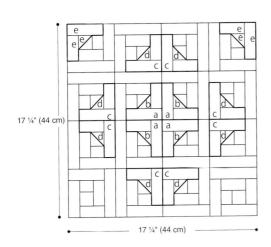

Block C (make 4)

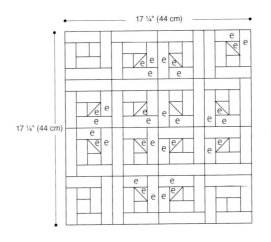

Fabric Layout Key
e: beige check
unlabeled: beige solid

5. Finish the quilt

Sew the blocks together in rows of four, following the layout indicated in the diagram below. Sew the six rows together to complete the quilt top. Cut the batting and backing so they are 6" (15 cm) larger than the quilt top. Layer the top, batting, and backing. Baste, then quilt along the center of each log cabin piece. Bind the bedspread using the rounded corner binding technique shown on pages 16-17.

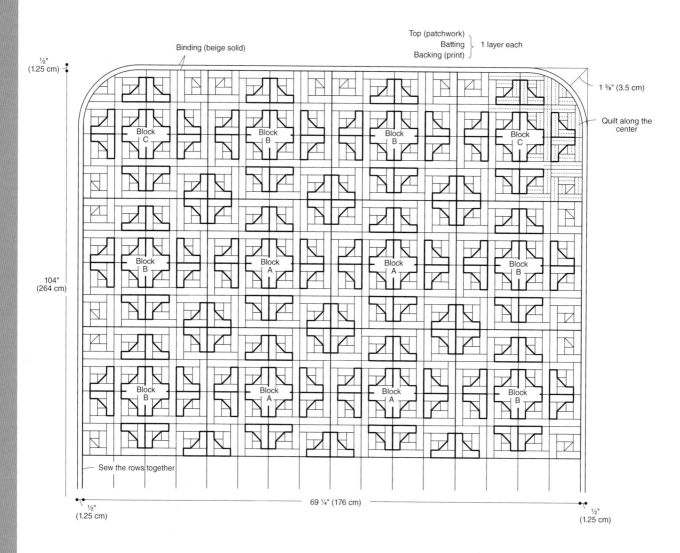

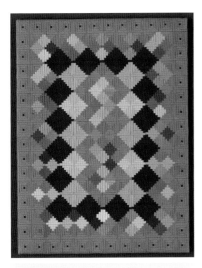

AMISH TAPESTRY

shown on page 122

Finished Size: 16 ½" x 22" (42 x 56 cm)

Note: *This project is designed with a cardboard insert for added support when hanging on a wall. Due to the cardboard insert, this tapestry is not quilted. You can always omit the cardboard insert and quilt the tapestry following the instructions on pages 14-16.*

RECOMMENDED CONSTRUCTION TECHNIQUE:

Method C:
Paper Piece...page 36

Materials

- 1259 ⅞" (3200 cm) of ⅝" (1.5 cm) wide strips of mauve solid cotton (for log cabin pieces)
- 16 ½" x 22" (42 x 56 cm) of mauve solid cotton (for backing)
- 4 ¼" x 42 ⅛" (11 x 107 cm) of mauve solid cotton (for back borders)
- 511 ⅞" (1300 cm) of ⅝" (1.5 cm) wide strips of maroon

solid cotton (for log cabin pieces)
- ⅝" (1.5 cm) wide strips of assorted purple, green, blue, and pink solid cottons (for log cabin pieces)
- 18 ⅞" x 23 ⅝" (48 x 60 cm) of batting
- One 16 ½" x 22" (42 x 56 cm) piece of ¼" (0.7 cm) thick cardboard
- Tracing paper

Sew using ¼" (0.5 cm) seam allowances, unless otherwise noted.

Construction Steps

1. Make the log cabin blocks

Cut out strips for the log cabin pieces. All strips should be ¼" (0.5 cm) wide without seam allowance. This means that the pieces will be ⅝" (1.5 cm) wide once the seam allowance has been added. Sew the pieces together in numerical order to make 52 of Pattern A and 140 of Pattern B. Refer to the diagram on page 154 for Pattern B fabric layouts.

Pattern A (make 52)

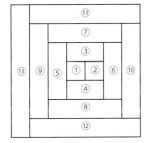

All pieces are ¼" (0.5 cm) wide.

PIECE	FABRIC
①	maroon
②~⑬	mauve

Pattern B (make 140)

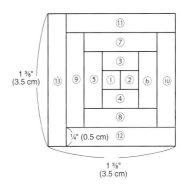

2. Make the quilt top

Follow the same process used in step 2 on page 59 to sew the Pattern B blocks together in groups of four. This will create 35 large blocks. Sew the large Pattern B blocks together in seven rows of five, as shown in the diagram below. Sew 12 Pattern A blocks together for each the top and bottom borders. Sew 14 Pattern A blocks together for each the left and right borders. Sew the borders to the assembled Pattern B blocks.

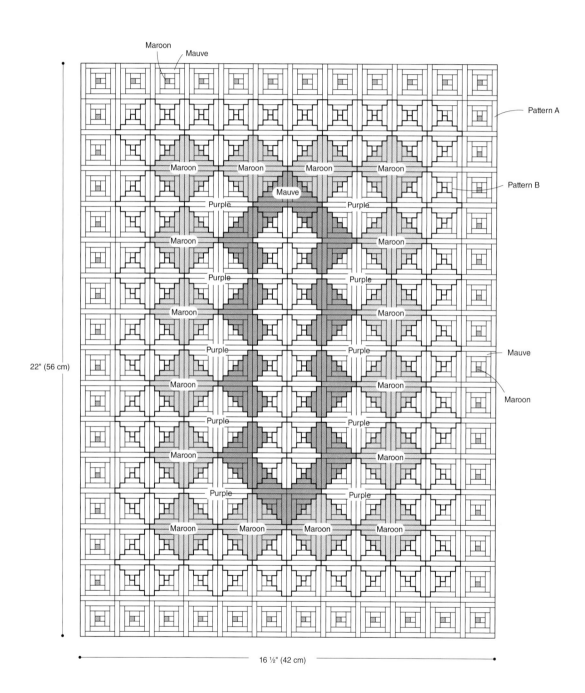

3. Add the back borders

Cut out the back border pieces according to the dimensions provided in the diagram at right, adding $^3/_8$" (1 cm) seam allowance. With right sides together, sew the back borders to the assembled blocks to complete the quilt top.

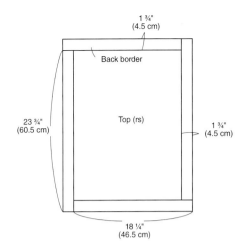

4. Layer the quilt components

Remove the foundation paper templates from the wrong side of the quilt top. Glue the wrong side of the backing to the cardboard insert using adhesive spray. Glue the batting to the other side of the cardboard insert, then layer the top over the batting.

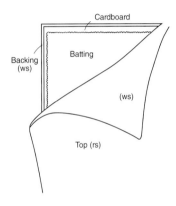

5. Finish the quilt

Use pushpins to hold the quilt flat while the spray adhesive dries. Fold the back border pieces to the back of the quilt and whipstitch to the backing.

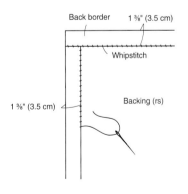

BOUTIS COASTERS

shown on page 124

Finished Size:
Variations 1-8: 3 1/8" x 3 1/8" (8 x 8 cm)
Variation 9: 8 3/8" x 8 3/8" (21.2 x 21.2 cm)

Full-size templates of Variations 1-8 are included on page 159. A full-size template of Variation 9 is located on Pattern Sheet A.

RECOMMENDED CONSTRUCTION TECHNIQUE:

Double-Sided Log Cabin Block...page 40

Materials & Tools (for one coaster)

- 23 5/8" x 23 5/8" (60 x 60 cm) of thin white cotton (for top, backing, log cabin pieces, and binding)
- 23 5/8" x 23 5/8" (60 x 60 cm) of batting
- Scraps of cotton yarn
- Boxwood needle
- Trapunto needle

- Wool needle
- Sewing needle
- Basting thread
- 60-90 weight cotton or polyester thread
- Tape
- Fabric safe mechanical pencil

Sew using 3/8" (1 cm) seam allowances, unless otherwise noted.

Construction Steps

1. Transfer the design to the fabric

Trace or copy the design onto paper, then tape to your work surface. For variations 1-8, cut out a 2 3/8" x 2 3/8" (6 x 6 cm) piece for the top (this measurement includes seam allowance). For variation 9, cut out a top piece using the template on Pattern Sheet A. Align the center of the fabric with the center of the template, then tape the fabric in place. Trace the design onto the fabric, starting at the center and working outwards. Cut out a piece of the same size for the backing. Align the fabric grains of the top and backing pieces, then baste together with right sides facing out.

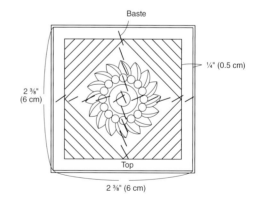

2. Running stitch the design

Using cotton or polyester thread, running stitch along the lines of the pattern using small stitches. Hide the knot between the two layers of fabric and make one backstitch when starting or ending a thread. Once the design has been running stitched, remove the basting.

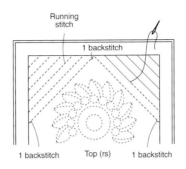

3. Stuff with yarn

Using a boxwood needle, make a small hole in the backing by opening the grain of the fabric. Use a trapunto needle to insert a piece of cotton yarn between the two layers of fabric. Trim the excess yarn and push the ends back in between the layers of fabric. Use a wool needle threaded with two strands of yarn to stuff the straight sections of each design. For these sections, insert the yarn at one end and draw it out at the other, as shown in the step 4 diagram.

4. Hide the yarn ends

Use a boxwood needle to gently press the fabric grain back into place and close the holes. For the straight sections, trim one end of the yarn even with the fabric and trim the other end, leaving ¼" (0.5 cm). Use a trapunto needle to insert the ends back in between the two layers of fabric.

Top (rs)

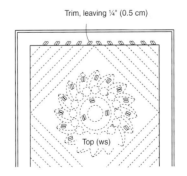

5. Make the double-sided log cabin block

Cut out strips for the log cabin pieces. All strips should be ⅛" (0.3 cm) wide without seam allowance. This means that the pieces will be ⅞" (2.3 cm) wide once seam allowance has been added. Follow the instructions on pages 40-41 to make a double-sided log cabin block around the design, using the dimensions provided in the diagram at right. Follow the instructions on pages 16-20 to bind the coaster. Note: Use the log cabin block motif in the diagram at right for variations 1-8 and the motif in the digram below for variation 9.

Variations 1-8

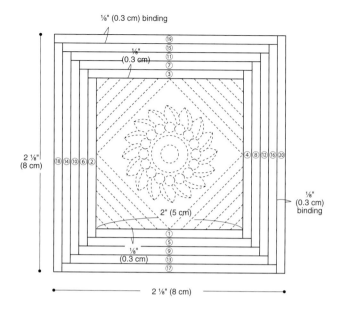

All pieces are ⅛" (0.3 cm) wide.

Variation 9

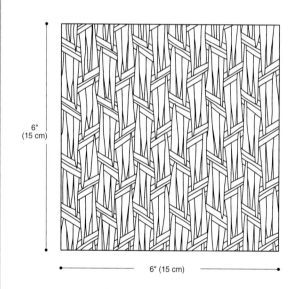

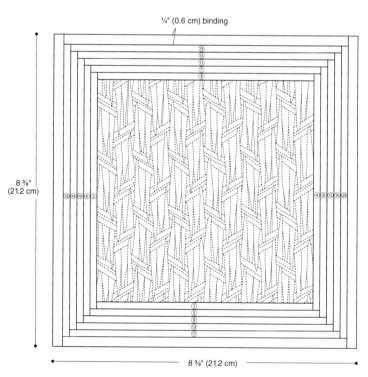

All pieces are ¼" (0.5 cm) wide.

Full-Size Templates

Variation 1

Variation 2

Variation 3

Variation 4

Variation 5

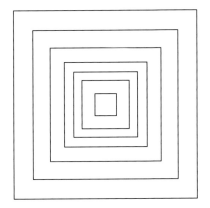

Variation 6

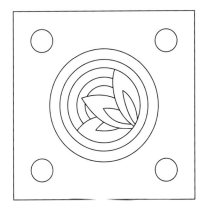

Variation 7

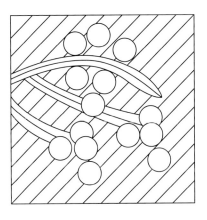

Variation 8

LANDSCAPE BLOCKS

shown on page 125

Finished Size:

Variation 1: 5″ x 6 ⁷/₈″ (12.5 x 17.5 cm)

Variation 2: 3 ³/₄″ x 5 ¹/₄″ (9.5 x 13.5 cm)

Note: This project is designed without batting or backing because it is meant to be framed. You can always add batting and backing, then finish the quilt following the instructions on pages 14-20.

RECOMMENDED CONSTRUCTION TECHNIQUE:

Method C:
Paper Piece...page 36

Materials

Variation 1
- Scraps of assorted print cottons (for log cabin pieces)
- 2 ³/₄″ x 13 ³/₄″ (7 x 35 cm) of black and white striped cotton (for borders)
- 6″ x 7 ⁷/₈″ (15 x 20 cm) of tracing paper

Variation 2
- Scraps of assorted print cottons (for log cabin pieces)
- 3 ¹/₈″ x 9 ³/₄″ (8 x 25 cm) of beige checked cotton (for borders)
- 4 ³/₄″ x 6 ¹/₄″ (12 x 16 cm) of tracing paper

Sew using ¹/₄″ (0.5 cm) seam allowances, unless otherwise noted.

Construction Steps

1. Make the foundation paper template
Draw the log cabin block following the dimensions indicated in the diagram on page 161 (refer to page 8 for instructions on drawing a log cabin block). Transfer the pattern onto tracing paper to create the foundation paper template.

2. Cut out the strips
Cut out strips for the log cabin pieces. All strips should be ¹/₄″-1″ (0.5-2.5 cm) wide without seam allowance. This means the pieces will be ⁵/₈″-1 ³/₈″ (1.5-3.5 cm) wide once seam allowance has been added.

3. Make the block
Sew the pieces together in numerical order using the paper piecing construction technique.

4. Add the borders
Cut out two border a pieces and two border b pieces for each block, following the dimensions indicated in the diagrams on page 161 (these measurements include seam allowance). Sew the borders to the block. Note: The back of this project is not finished because it is designed to be displayed in a frame. As a result, there's no need to remove the foundation paper templates from the wrong side.

Variation 1

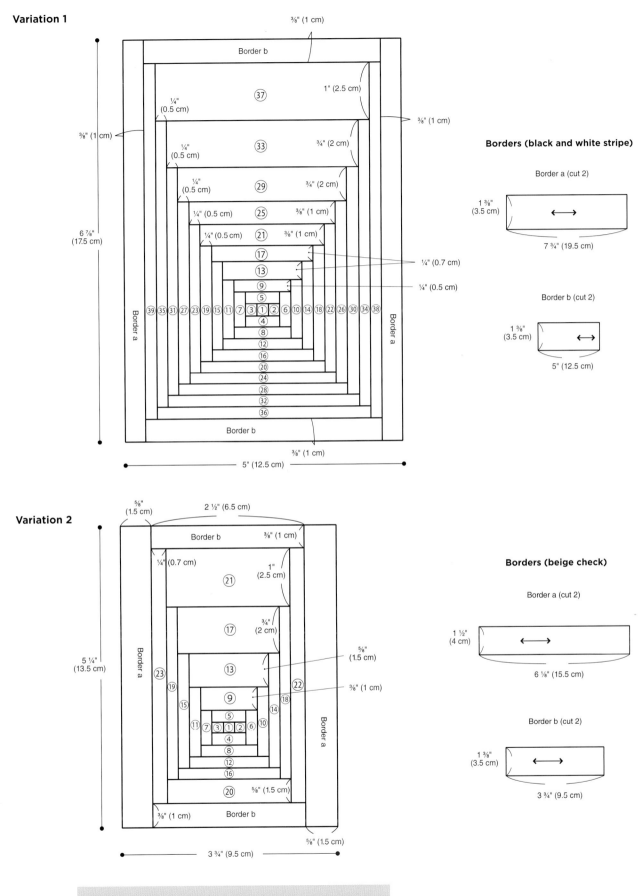

³⁄₈" (1 cm)

Border b

1" (2.5 cm)

37

¼" (0.5 cm)

³⁄₈" (1 cm)

¼" (0.5 cm)

33

¾" (2 cm)

¼" (0.5 cm)

29

¾" (2 cm)

³⁄₈" (1 cm)

25

³⁄₈" (1 cm)

¼" (0.5 cm)

21

³⁄₈" (1 cm)

¼" (0.5 cm)

17

¼" (0.7 cm)

13

¼" (0.5 cm)

9

5

39 35 31 27 23 19 15 11 7 3 1 2 6 10 14 18 22 26 30 34 38

4

8

12

16

20

24

28

32

36

Border b

³⁄₈" (1 cm)

³⁄₈" (1 cm)

6 ⁷⁄₈" (17.5 cm)

Border a

Border a

5" (12.5 cm)

Borders (black and white stripe)

Border a (cut 2)

1 ³⁄₈" (3.5 cm)

←→

7 ¾" (19.5 cm)

Border b (cut 2)

1 ³⁄₈" (3.5 cm)

←→

5" (12.5 cm)

Variation 2

⁵⁄₈" (1.5 cm)

2 ½" (6.5 cm)

Border b

³⁄₈" (1 cm)

¼" (0.7 cm)

21

1" (2.5 cm)

17

¾" (2 cm)

13

⁵⁄₈" (1.5 cm)

9

³⁄₈" (1 cm)

5

23 19 15 11 7 3 1 2 6 10 14 18 22

4

8

12

16

20 ⁵⁄₈" (1.5 cm)

Border b

³⁄₈" (1 cm)

⁵⁄₈" (1.5 cm)

5 ¼" (13.5 cm)

Border a

Border a

3 ¾" (9.5 cm)

Borders (beige check)

Border a (cut 2)

1 ½" (4 cm)

←→

6 ⅛" (15.5 cm)

Border b (cut 2)

1 ³⁄₈" (3.5 cm)

←→

3 ¾" (9.5 cm)

All pieces are ¼" (0.5 cm) wide, unless otherwise noted.

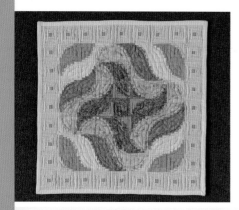

WAVE & LEAF TAPESTRIES

shown on page 126

Finished Size:

Variation 1:

18 ³/₄" x 18 ³/₄" (47.5 x 47.5 cm)

Variation 2:

20 ³/₄" x 20 ³/₄" (52.5 x 52.5 cm)

RECOMMENDED CONSTRUCTION TECHNIQUE:

Method B: Machine Stitch...page 34

Materials

Variation 1

- 7 ⁷/₈" x 11 ³/₄" (20 x 30 cm) of pink print calico (for log cabin pieces)
- 7 ⁷/₈" x 11 ³/₄" (20 x 30 cm) of blue print calico (for log cabin pieces)
- 11 ³/₄" x 15 ³/₄" (30 x 40 cm) of beige and blue print calico (for log cabin pieces)
- 11 ³/₄" x 13 ³/₄" (30 x 35 cm) of blue solid cotton (for log cabin pieces)
- 23 ⁵/₈" x 35 ¹/₂" (60 x 90 cm) of beige solid cotton (for log cabin pieces)
  - Includes 78 ³/₄" (200 cm) of 1 ¹/₂" (4 cm) wide bias strips (for binding)
- 21 ³/₄" x 21 ³/₄" (55 x 55 cm) of beige print cotton (for backing)
- 21 ³/₄" x 21 ³/₄" (55 x 55 cm) of batting

Variation 2

- 11 ³/₄" x 11 ³/₄" (30 x 30 cm) of dark brown print calico (for log cabin pieces)
- 11 ³/₄" x 15 ³/₄" (30 x 40 cm) of golden brown print calico (for log cabin pieces)
- 11 ³/₄" x 27 ¹/₂" (30 x 70 cm) of tan solid cotton (for log cabin pieces)
- 23 ⁵/₈" x 35 ¹/₂" (60 x 90 cm) of beige solid cotton (for log cabin pieces)
  - Includes 86 ⁵/₈" (220 cm) of 1 ¹/₂" (4 cm) wide bias strips (for binding)
- 23 ⁵/₈" x 23 ⁵/₈" (60 x 60 cm) of beige floral print cotton (for backing)
- 23 ⁵/₈" x 23 ⁵/₈" (60 x 60 cm) of batting

Sew using ¹/₄" (0.5 cm) seam allowances, unless otherwise noted.

Construction Steps

1. Make the log cabin blocks

Cut out strips for the log cabin pieces. Without seam allowance, the strips should be ¹/₄" (0.5 cm) or ³/₈" (1 cm) wide. This means that the pieces will be ⁵/₈" (1.5 cm) or ³/₄" (2 cm) wide once the seam allowance has been added. Sew the pieces together in numerical order to make 33 of Pattern A and 48 of Pattern B for Variation 1 or 44 of Pattern A and 56 of Pattern B for Variation 2.

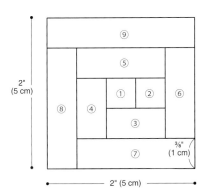

Pattern A

(Variation 1: make 33

Variation 2: make 44)

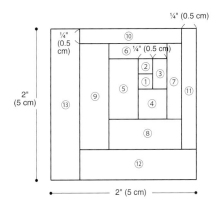

Pattern B

(Variation 1: make 48

Variation 2: make 56)

All pieces are ³⁄₈" (1 cm) wide, unless otherwise noted.

VARIATION	PIECE	FABRIC
1	①	blue solid cotton
2	①	golden brown print calico
1 & 2	②-⑨	beige solid cotton

2. Sew the blocks together

Sew the blocks together to complete the quilt top, following the layout indicated in the diagrams below.

Variation 1

Variation 2

3. Finish the quilt

Cut the batting and backing so they are 6" (15 cm) larger than the quilt top. Layer the top, batting, and backing. Baste, then quilt as shown in the diagram below. Follow the instructions on pages 16-20 to bind the quilt.

Unlabeled log cabin blocks are Pattern B

Variation 1

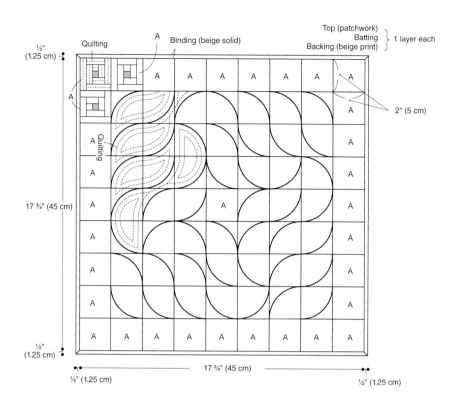

Variation 2

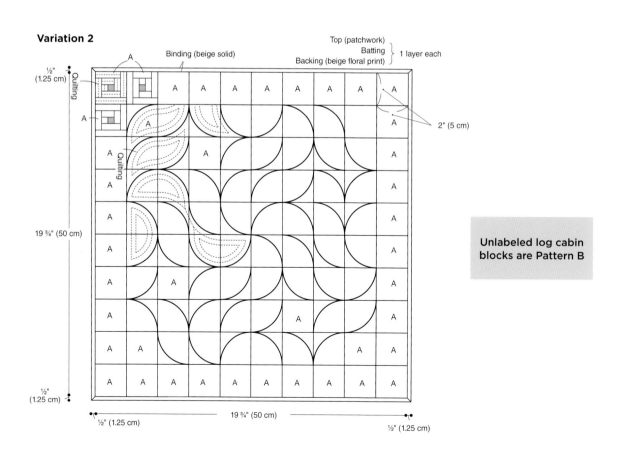

Unlabeled log cabin blocks are Pattern B

FLYING VULTURE TAPESTRY

shown on page 127

Finished Size: 67 ⅛" x 67 ⅛" (170.5 x 170.5 cm)

RECOMMENDED CONSTRUCTION TECHNIQUE:

Method B: Machine Stitch...page 34

Materials

- a: 35 ½" x 118 ⅛" (90 x 300 cm) of red plaid cotton (for log cabin pieces)
- b: 11 ¾" x 51 ¼" (30 x 130 cm) of beige print cotton (for log cabin pieces)
- c: 11 ¾" x 126" (30 x 320 cm) of beige solid cotton (for log cabin pieces)
- d: 11 ¾" x 39 ⅜" (30 x 100 cm) of maroon print cotton (for log cabin pieces)

- e: 11 ¾" x 366 ⅛" (30 x 930 cm) of maroon solid cotton (for log cabin pieces)
  - Includes 271 ¾" (690 cm) of 1 ¾" (4.5 cm) wide bias strips (for binding)
- 49 ¼" x 137 ⅞" (125 x 350 cm) of maroon large print cotton (for backing)
- 49 ¼" x 137 ⅞" (125 x 350 cm) of batting

Sew using ¼" (0.6 cm) seam allowances, unless otherwise noted.

Construction Steps

1. Make the Pattern A log cabin blocks

Cut out strips for the log cabin pieces. All strips should be ⅝" (1.5 cm) wide without seam allowance. This means that the pieces will be 1 ⅛" (2.7 cm) wide once seam allowance has been added. Sew the pieces together in numerical order to make 188 Pattern A blocks.

Pattern A (make 188)

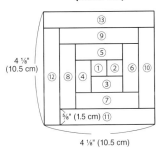

4 ⅛" (10.5 cm)

4 ⅛" (10.5 cm)

⅝" (1.5 cm)

All pieces are ⅝" (1.5 cm) wide.

BLOCK QUANTITY	PIECES	FABRIC
60	① ②–⑫	c: beige solid e: maroon solid
20	①④⑤⑧⑨⑫⑬ ②③⑥⑦⑩⑪	d: maroon print e: maroon solid
20	①④⑤⑧⑨⑫⑬ ②③⑥⑦⑩⑪	a: red plaid e: maroon solid
16	①②③⑩⑪ ⑥⑦ ④⑤⑧⑨⑫⑬	b: beige print c: beige solid e: maroon solid
16	①④⑤⑧⑨⑫⑬ ⑥⑦ ②⑧⑩⑪	a: red plaid b: beige print c: beige solid
40	①④⑤⑧⑨⑫⑬ ②③⑥⑦⑩⑪	c: beige solid a: red plaid
12	①④⑤⑧⑨⑫⑬ ②③⑥⑦⑩⑪	c: beige solid d: maroon print

2. Make the Pattern B log cabin blocks

Make templates for pieces ① and ②. Cut out the pieces, adding ¼" (0.6 cm) seam allowance. Cut out strips for the remaining log cabin pieces. All strips should be ⅝" (1.5 cm) wide without seam allowance. This means that the pieces will be 1 ⅛" (2.7 cm) wide once seam allowance has been added. Sew the pieces together in numerical order to make 16 Pattern B blocks.

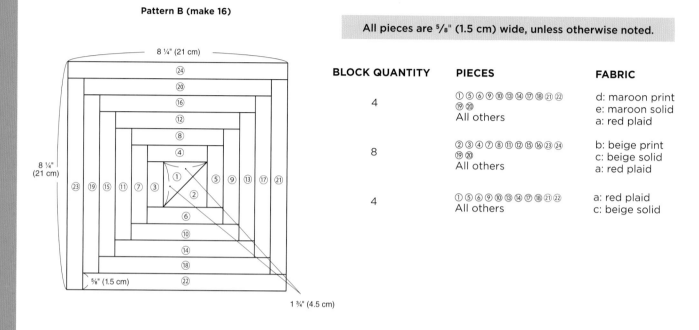

Pattern B (make 16)

All pieces are ⅝" (1.5 cm) wide, unless otherwise noted.

BLOCK QUANTITY	PIECES	FABRIC
4	① ⑤ ⑥ ⑨ ⑩ ⑬ ⑭ ⑰ ⑱ ㉑ ㉒ ⑲ ⑳ All others	d: maroon print e: maroon solid a: red plaid
8	② ③ ④ ⑦ ⑧ ⑪ ⑫ ⑮ ⑯ ㉓ ㉔ ⑲ ⑳ All others	b: beige print c: beige solid a: red plaid
4	① ⑤ ⑥ ⑨ ⑩ ⑬ ⑭ ⑰ ⑱ ㉑ ㉒ All others	a: red plaid c: beige solid

3. Make the Pattern C log cabin block

Make a template for piece ①. Cut out the piece on the bias, adding ¼" (0.6 cm) seam allowance. Cut out strips for the remaining log cabin pieces. All strips should be ⅝" (1.5 cm) wide without seam allowance. This means that the pieces will be 1 ⅛" (2.7 cm) wide once seam allowance has been added. Sew the pieces together in numerical order to make one Pattern C block.

Pattern C (make 1)

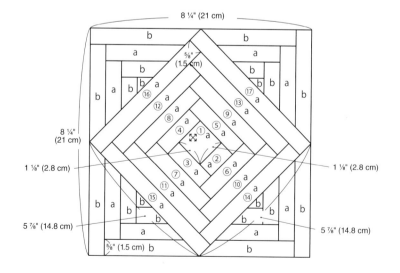

All pieces are ⅝" (1.5 cm) wide, unless otherwise noted.

4. Sew the quilt together

Sew the Pattern A, B, and C blocks together, following the layout provided in the diagram below. Cut the batting and backing so they are 6" (15 cm) larger than the quilt top. Layer the top, batting, and backing. Baste, then quilt along the center of each log cabin piece and around the outline of the the triangular pieces. Follow the instructions on pages 16-20 to bind the quilt.

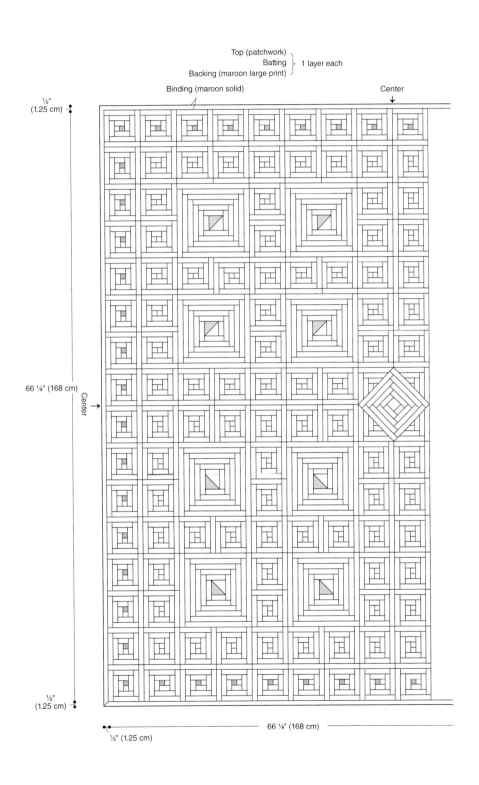

Top (patchwork)
Batting } 1 layer each
Backing (maroon large print)

Binding (maroon solid)

Center

½" (1.25 cm)

66 ⅛" (168 cm)

Center

½" (1.25 cm)

66 ⅛" (168 cm)

½" (1.25 cm)

ABOUT THE AUTHOR

Shizuko Kuroha first discovered the joy of quilting in the 1970s when she spent two years living in the United States in Maryland. Upon returning home to Japan she began teaching classes and is credited as a key figure who helped make quilting popular in Japan. Kuroha is famous for her use of traditional Japanese indigo fabric and her work is exhibited around the world. She is the owner of a quilt studio called Nuno Space in Tokyo and the author of more than 30 books. Her books have been translated into English, German and French. You can learn more about Shizuko Kuroha her website: www.kuroha.com.